Challenge to The New God
The Resistance to Nuclear Weapons

Compiled and edited by

DON MASON
and
CATHERINE ROBINSON (Quaker)

Gooday
Publishers

303.61.

First Published by Gooday Publishers
P.O. Box 60, East Wittering, West Sussex PO20 8RA

© 1988 Don Mason and Catherine Robinson

(Quaker)

British Library Cataloguing in Publication Data

Challenge to the new god: the
  resistance to nuclear weapons
1. Pacifism
I. Mason, Don and Robinson, Catherine
327. 1'72

ISBN 1−870568−09−5

Typeset in Times by Woodfield Graphics, Fontwell, West Sussex.
Printed in Great Britain by Hollen Street Press, Slough, Berks.

Contents

The supreme trick of mass insanity is that it persuades you that the only abnormal person is the one who refuses to join in the madness of others, the one who tries vainly to resist.

Eugene Ionesco

This book is dedicated to the many people whose support, both moral and practical, make it possible for others openly to challenge the design, construction and deployment of nuclear weapons.

Introduction

Life exists on earth; it emerged about three billion years ago. Before the event of life, the chances that it would occur were exceedingly small. Furthermore, from our understanding of the probable manner in which our present atmosphere evolved, and of the critical part played by living organisms in this process, it seems the decisive event - the transition from non-living to living matter - occurred once, and could occur only once.

(Sir Bernard Lovell: *In the Centre of Immensities*)

We live, year by year, in a period unique in the history of life on earth. For the human race has developed the capacity to turn much of the earth's surface into a radioactive wasteland, devoid of all but the most primitive forms of life. Now, in the Northern Hemisphere at least, we can reverse in a few hours or days what evolution has taken billions of years to establish. It seems that our scientific and technological development has outstripped our capacity to deal wisely with what we have discovered. However, if the threat to our survival is of our own making, then the answer to this threat is also in our own hands.

Although self-evident, this statement poses the crucial question of how we are to extricate ourselves from our precarious position. Given our past history and the present destructive power that we have so painstakingly developed, it is perhaps easy to adopt a pessimistic view and conclude that we shall fail to find a solution to the problem we have made for ourselves.

However, only the most hardened cynic would deny that we have made significant moral and social progress in recorded history. For example, slave labour which built the Parthenon in Athens and the pyramids at Giza is no longer acceptable in most parts of the world

1

today and we no longer crucify common thieves. This is not to deny that there are temporary but sometimes gross reversals of this upward trend. The holocaust that occurred in the present century is an example of the fact that reactionary forces can be powerful enough to capture a highly civilized country like Germany and turn it into an instrument of mass murder. Despite these reversals, the overall trend gives cause for hope. However, social change does not come about spontaneously: the abolition of slavery and of child labour, advances in prison reform, the emancipation of women, and the many other social changes that are all evidence of our moral progress have come about because, in each case, a few heretical individuals have challenged a situation, and by their example have encouraged others to do the same.

Heretics are not generally made welcome, especially by those in authority. The pagan orthodoxy of ancient Rome responded to the Christian heresy with violent suppression, similar to the reaction of the British Raj in India when faced with Gandhi's declaration that India belonged to its native population. Similarly Martin Luther King encountered hostility from the dominant white population when he roused the black people in Alabama to the realization that they merited parity with their white neighbours. It should be noted that, with rare exceptions, the opposition to change in these instances was within the law as it existed at the time. Indeed by its very nature the law resists change. As West Germany judge, Ulf Panzer, explains:

'Law in its operation is a conservative thing. It functions to keep the status quo. It is an instrument of power, really. It is rarely that law changes the opinion of Society. It's almost always the other way round: that Society changes, and the law follows.'

It is, of course, easy to see from this statement that those pressing for social change may come into conflict with the law as it exists at the time. Where this has come about in the past, the outcome has depended very much on the qualities of the individuals who see the need for change most acutely. In the case of India in the years before independence, and in the Civil Rights movement in the United States in the 1960s, leaders emerged who, while openly challenging the law, achieved their objectives by non-violent means. It should be stressed here that non-violent does not mean passive. In fact 'passive resistance' was not a term that met with Gandhi's approval.[1] A better term - non-violent direct action - has been described by Martin Luther King in the following way:

2

'Non-violent direct action seeks to create such a crisis and foster such a tension that a community which has constantly refused to negotiate is forced to confront the issue. It seeks so to dramatise the issue that it can no longer be ignored. My citing the creation of tension as part of the work of the non-violent resister may sound rather shocking. But I must confess that I am not afraid of the word 'tension'. I have earnestly opposed violent tension, but there is a type of constructive, non-violent tension which is necessary for growth.'

Social progress brought about in this way may exact a heavy price from those who seek to achieve it: they must be prepared to suffer for what they believe in. However, the durability of the gains won by these means is very much in evidence - once a step forward has been made, reversals, if they occur, are short-lived. The Roman empire has long since disappeared - Christianity, for all its bloodstained faults in the past, is still with us.

This book is a collection of writings by modern heretics. They have, by non-violent means, challenged the orthodox view that nuclear weapons are morally acceptable because they offer some sort of security to those who possess them. As with heretics in the past, they are dealt with harshly by those who accept the current orthodoxy. Like other heretics, they have made no attempts to avoid the punitive legal consequences of their actions, but have instead accepted them as essential for the generation of the constructive non-violent tension of which King speaks.

Some of the American contributors to this book are members of a loosely-knit group of peace protesters called the 'Plowshare and Pruning Hooks' activists. They take their title from some verses in the book of Isaiah:

'They shall beat their swords into Ploughshares, and their spears into pruning hooks: nation shall not lift up sword against nation, neither shall they learn war any more.' Isaiah Ch.2:4.

In a number of instances these activists have hammered on nuclear weapons installations in symbolic attempts to bring the prophecy in Isaiah to fruition. Their objective, of course, has been to bring into public awareness the fallacy of the belief that anything of moral worth can be protected by instruments of genocide. The physical damage caused by their hammering has been relatively minor, but sentences of 18 years in prison (later reduced to 12 years) have been passed in some cases. It may be argued that the actions have not been non-violent because material damage has been caused. This criticism is answered with wonderful clarity by one of the writers in this book:

'What exactly is a missile launch facility? Is it property as we normally understand the term property, the way a kitchen stove or a bicycle is property? Or is it the ultimate expression of a human impulse for destruction, a weapon that is anti-property, anti-life?'

Most peace activists outside the United States have been arrested for either cutting perimeter fences around nuclear weapons bases or for attempting to interrupt the function of these bases by obstruction of the roads into them. Occasionally mass human blockades of military bases have resulted in their temporary isolation, but in most instances the actions, like those in the United States, have been symbolic rather than material. One form of peace witness that is becoming increasingly common in the United Kingdom is the conscientious withholding of the proportion of one's income tax that is levied for military purposes. One contributor to this book is the first peace tax campaigner to be imprisoned for an attempt to divert his 'defence' taxes to expenditure on social welfare.

In inviting peace activists to contribute to this book we have used only one criterion - namely that the individuals have been imprisoned for their actions. Consequently, apart from this feature, the selection may be regarded as a random one. Bearing this fact in mind it is notable that all the contributors have certain features in common. All the activists have, not surprisingly, been well informed about the facts pertaining to the arms race. More significant, the contributors have all spent a considerable length of time in deciding to take the steps that they did - none acted on impulse. Instead they have examined the possibility that other, less demanding, actions might achieve their objectives. Having concluded that no real alternatives exist, they have acted with quiet resolution, not only during the actions themselves but afterwards, in court and in prison.

In contrast to these common characteristics, the contributors have shown a range of religious convictions - some are Catholics, one a Jew, another would probably describe herself as an agnostic, and another as a Universalist. However even here common features may be perceived. All show concern for humanity at large; they appear not to be motivated by personal fear of nuclear weapons but rather by what these weapons may do to life, regardless of race, nationality, or creed.

4

One less attractive feature is commonly encountered in these writings and is, in fact, a frequent experience of those arrested for non-violent direct action. Judges trying such cases have most often instructed juries to disregard the testimony of defendants where it relates to the ethical case against nuclear weapons or the possible status of these weapons under International Law. In some cases defendants have been forbidden to present expert witnesses to testify on these matters. It is a sobering thought that the law puts on trial those who protest against weapons of mass destruction, while ruling as irrelevant any testimony bearing on the issue of whether the possession of these weapons is either morally acceptable or even legal under International Law.

It is easy to see the corrosive effect that the arms race has on the nations who participate in it, and to see how, as in the past, law may impede social change. While collecting material for this book the editors have inevitably come to compare the treatment of peace activists in different countries. As noted, some similarities are apparent. However the treatment of members of the Turkish Peace Association stands apart as characterised by gross violation of human rights. The article by one member of this association now living in exile in England is without doubt the most disturbing in the book.

The act of going to prison implies much more than the loss of physical freedom. Imprisonment may turn a two-parent family into a one-parent one or deprive a partner of a breadwinner's earnings. It is not surprising that peace protesters, especially those contemplating acts of civil disobedience likely to incur long prison sentences, have given much careful thought to the possible pain that their actions may cause others. It says much for the peace movement that the relatives of those going to prison have been so willing to make their own, less noticeable, contributions to the protest.

What impact the actions of these peace protesters will have on future events remains to be seen. The objective they have set themselves, to encourage nations to establish a peace based on trust and compassion, rather than on a balance of terror, seems remote at present. However, if the human race is to justify its place here, we must ultimately reject the weapons of mass destruction that have the capacity to render sterile much of the Earth's surface. If, instead, we turn our efforts towards nurturing the planet on which we find ourselves, then we will become worthy of our own place in an awe-inspiring creation that our intellect can hardly begin to comprehend.

Notes

1. Gandhi coined the word 'satyagraha', literally truth-force or love-force. According to this concept the opposition must be 'weaned from error by patience and sympathy'. A Buddhist parable that concludes with the statement 'Hatred is not overcome by hatred, hatred is overcome by love', expresses the same idea. There seem to have been some notable converts to a belief in Satyagraha. General Douglas MacArthur, supreme Allied Commander in Japan at the end of World War II commented, on hearing of Gandhi's death:

    'In the evolution of civilization, if it is to survive, all men cannot fail eventually to adopt Gandhi's belief that the process of mass application of force to resolve contentious issues is fundamentally not only wrong but contains within it the germs of self-destruction'.

CHAPTER ONE

Obedience?

MARTIN HOLLADAY

Martin Holladay is a thirty year old Roman Catholic carpenter who lives in a house that he built himself in the woods of the state of Vermont, USA. He comes from a remarkable family. His sister was killed in the act of saving her own and her neighbours' children from a runaway car, and his 57-year-old mother Jean, a psychiatric nurse who speaks Spanish and Dutch as well as English, has served a one-year prison sentence for damaging six Trident II nuclear missile tubes at the Quonset Point Shipyard in 1984. Martin, his mother, and his sister Cathy, who was killed by the runaway car, all took part in anti-Vietnam War protests in 1972. In February 1985 Martin received an eight-year prison sentence for damaging the lid of a nuclear missile silo in Missouri. He was released in September 1986 but remains on probation until 1991.

This article was written while he was in prison.

Sometimes I am asked, 'Why do you choose civil disobedience?' I answer in various ways—'Because nuclear weapons have brought us to a crisis', 'Because one must heed the call of conscience', and so on—but I am often tempted to turn the question around, and to ask, 'What madness has seized us that we are so obedient?'

Here in the USA there is an enormous conspiracy afoot, operating in hundreds of factories in every state of the union—a conspiracy to build and deploy three to five new nuclear warheads every day. The nuclear arms race has necessitated a deliberate diversion of resources away from productive enterprises, and an application of ingenuity probably unparalleled in human history. The expenditure of effort required to sustain the arms race would make it appear to be one of the supreme flowers of the national will.

This production machine operates virtually unhindered by resistance from the citizenry. Those who have decided to produce these weapons are mad; and the madness extends to all of us who in the face of this scheme choose silence, which is a kind of complicity. We are playing out the wild drama of the suicide of the species in lock-step, in an inexplicable nightmare of obedience.

We remain obedient at the risk of our lives – for continued obedience to the nuclear states will lead us to the predictable holocaust. What is worse (for there are times when we must choose to risk our lives), we remain obedient at the risk of our very souls. We pay for the false protection of the Bomb with the willingness to perform unprecedented murder. The logic of the arms race attempts to declare morality irrelevant, as if technological advances could erase the distinction between good and evil. We choose resistance not because it is effective (although I believe it is), but because it is right.

It is testimony to the great failure of the Christian community that there is any necessity to explain this. As Christians we are called to love our enemies; we cannot begin to live that love as long as we are armed. To be armed is to threaten to kill. Disarmament is the starting point of our lives as Christians – we who follow the way of Jesus, God disarmed and hanging on the cross.

Taking actual steps toward disarmament is not an easy task. We do not see disarmament occuring within the legal structure, which has institutionalised war. As Plowshares activists have discovered, disarmament is profoundly suspect, directly at odds with the intention of government, and illegal.

Personally, I avoided the call to civil disobedience for several years. For a while there was a tug-of-war in my conscience between my growing sense of responsibility for the arms race and 'the cares and riches and pleasures of this life' (Luke 8:14). Eventually I began to realise that by inaction I risked not only my self-respect, which rationalisations could attempt to buttress, but even the likelihood of the continued enjoyment of worldly pleasures, all of which fall under the shadow of the Bomb. I began to see the smooth functioning of the machinery of the arms race, like the smooth functioning of the Nazi death camps, as a moral indictment of the citizenry, an indictment both general and personal. Before this analogy my own rationalisations for inaction collapsed.

My inability to accept the logic of the nuclear arms race is informed, of course, by my faith in non-violence: my faith that only love and forgiveness have the power to absorb and overcome the suicidal cycle of violence in which this world is apparently locked. Gandhi struggled with the limitations of various words and phrases to describe this power — *ahimsa*, non-violence, and passive resistance, for instance — all of which seemed to connote merely a failure to murder. He coined the word *satyagraha*, 'truth force', partly because it implies action rather than passivity. The path of *satyagraha*, the belief in the power of love and forgiveness, carries with it a responsibility to intervene in defence of the victims of injustice.

On February 19, 1985, I went alone to a Minuteman II missile launch facility in Missouri. There are about a thousand Minuteman missiles in the USA, deployed in underground silos scattered among farms and ranches. Each silo is relatively inconspicuous: the passing motorist sees only a level area, about a hundred yards square, surrounded by a chain-link fence. Inside are a few steel poles and the circular concrete slab which is the silo's moveable lid.

In what has become a familiar Plowshares ritual, I beat on the silo's lid with a hammer and poured blood on the concrete. After fifteen minutes, several vehicles full of security officers, alerted by electronic alarms, arrived to arrest me.

That afternoon I was taken before a magistrate for a bail hearing, at which my willingness to appear for trial was doubted. As a later official report explained, 'the defendant was found to be a potential flight risk and a danger to the community at the conclusion of this hearing. He was ordered detained without bail, pending trial.'

I decided to represent myself *pro se* at the trial, which opened about two months after my arrest. The trial was held in Room 666 of the U.S. District Courthouse in Kansas City, Missouri. Two armed U.S. Marshals were dispatched every morning to the jail, about twenty minutes' drive away, to bring me in handcuffs to court. The jury trial lasted four days.

In the government's opening statement, Assistant U.S. Attorney Daniel Stewart told the jury:*[1]

> On February 19, 1985, the defendant, Martin Holladay, attempted what he termed a disarmament action at a missile silo in Lafayette

9

County, Missouri. Based on that attempted disarmament action, he is charged with two offences. One is attempting to interfere with the national defence – that is, the destruction of national defence property; and two, damage to government property in excess of $100.

The evidence will show that on the morning of February 19, 1985, the defendant ... climbed the fence at missile silo N-11, referred to in military terms as 'November Eleven', located in Lafayette County. Armed with hand tools he brought with him – a hammer, screw-driver, chisel, a few other tools – he damaged some of the electrical and other equipment on the site. In all, he did somewhat over a thousand dollars in damage to the equipment. He was on the site for approximately fifteen minutes before the Air Force security police arrived and arrested him.

The missile site which Holladay entered was one of approximately 150 missile sites at Whiteman Air Force Base. They have those missile sites throughout central Missouri, and they are not controlled at each site. There is one control site, a launch control facility, which controls ten different sites. The control facility for this one was called N-1 – or, again as military people refer to it, 'November One'. That control facility is some miles away.

At the conclusion of the prosecutor's remarks, I made my own opening statement to the jury.

As we speak today, there is a sword over our heads, the sword of nuclear annihilation. The imminent danger of nuclear war is no longer a matter of speculation or science fiction. This danger is now a fact, because we know there are more than 40,000 nuclear weapons deployed over the face of the earth, ready in a matter of hours to vaporize every major city in the world, and to plunge the unlucky survivors into a nuclear winter from which no one can hope to recover. The farmland of central Missouri is filled with these weapons. In our hearts, in our dreams, in the back of our minds, we all know that this danger exists. Our children know it, too, and our children are afraid.

The main issue before you, the jury, in this trial is the legitimacy of these weapons of final destruction. How the human race decides this issue will determine whether the children in school today will ever know adulthood...

I came to Missouri to begin the process of taking responsibility for these weapons, to begin the process of disarmament... The evidence will show that on the morning of February 19, I entered the grounds of the Minuteman II missile silo called N-11. The missile silo was unmanned and unguarded... I tied up a cloth banner there, a banner which read, 'Swords into Plowshares'. This is a quote from the Bible, from Isaiah 2:4, where it is written:

'They shall beat their swords into plowshares
and their spears into pruning-hooks;

nation shall not lift up sword against nation,
neither shall they learn war anymore.'

... With a hammer and chisel I chipped some of the concrete on the
lid of the missile silo, and I damaged some other pieces of hardware
with a hammer. I also poured a quantity of blood onto the concrete lid
of the silo from a plastic baby bottle.
... I then stood by my banner to take responsibility for what I had
done. I waited around in case anyone wanted to come arrest me. People
did come and arrest me, and since then I have been held in Wyandotte
County Jail awaiting trial...

I do not intend to argue that a person is justified in damaging
property with a hammer just because he doesn't approve of the
property. That would be mere vandalism. My action came after a
long period of reflection and deliberation, and it was a difficult action
for me to take...

My action arose from the pondering of two questions. The first
question I pondered was: What exactly is a missile launch facility?
Is it property as we normally understand the term property, the way a
kitchen stove or a bicycle is property? Or is it the ultimate expression
of a human impulse for destruction, a weapon that is anti-property,
anti-life? All that we hold dear – our loved ones and all the genuine
property which enhances life – is held hostage by this weapon, this
demonic invention.

The second question I pondered is: Is our society now acting rationally
to face this gigantic threat, this crisis of survival? Does the spectre of
nuclear war shock us towards action, towards true disarmament, where
our only real security lies? The more I studied this, the more I discovered
that in fact our society is engaged in an escalating, accelerating arms
race, which is a form of madness. We are rushing towards oblivion...

My action is clearly a warning of danger and a call for help. It is also
an offering or sacrifice in the spirit of non-violence. I accept the risks of
my action out of my earnest prayer that people will listen to my call.

It is also a symbolic action, using the Christian symbol of blood
– which is a mysterious sign, both a sign of violence which tears us
apart, and a saving fluid which redeems us – and using the symbol of
the hammer, which is the emblem of disarmament as called for by the
prophet Isaiah.

It is also an action which attempts to speak a truth not only
through words, which can confuse and mislead, but through deeds.
My deed speaks to the illegitimacy of this weapon, and to the essential
need for true disarmament, which we can no longer afford to delay. My
action speaks to hope: the hope that we are not powerless in the face of
this danger.

One of the first witnesses which the prosecution chose to call to the
stand was Second Lieutenant Kevin Pollock of the U.S. Air Force,

who works at launch control facility N-1, several miles away from the silo where I was arrested. He is a man with unusual responsibilities.

U.S. Attorney Stewart: Could you please explain to the jury what your duties are as Deputy Combat Crew Commander?

Lt. Pollock: My primary duty is to turn keys if we get a message to launch the missiles...

Q: Can you give us a general description of what the launch control facility N-1, or November-One, looks like?

A: There is what we call the soft support building upstairs: just a building that has a kitchen; a couple of bedrooms; it has an area, a security area, called the S.E.C. And then you go down an elevator, and there are two buildings downstairs: the launch control equipment building, and the launch control centre. The launch control centre is where we pull our hours...

Q: Describe generally what your control capsule looks like, that you work in.

A: It is approximately 25 feet long. I would say it is about eight to ten feet wide. It has computer racks on the right side; a status indicator panel at the very front. On the left side there is a single bed. There is an oven, refrigerator — a small oven, a toaster oven: not a range. And there is an emergency air-conditioner on that site also. That is basically what it is.

Q: During the 24-hour duty you pull, you remain underground. Is that right?

A: Yes, sir.

After Lieutenant Pollock finished his direct testimony, I had the opportunity to cross-examine him.

Holladay: You said, if I remember correctly, that one of your duties was to turn the key when you get the message to launch. Is that basically correct?

Lt. Pollock: That is correct.

Q: This is what laypeople call 'pushing the button', isn't it?

A: Yes.

This man, working deep underground beside his emergency air-conditioner, which he is ready to turn on in case things get too hot, responsible for unleashing destruction on a scale that few of us have the courage to contemplate. One theme running through Lt. Pollock's answers to my questions was professed ignorance of the implications of his job: whether this was genuine naiveté, or was disingenuousness brought on by the military tendency towards secrecy and a disinclination to appear cooperative, is only to be guessed.

Q: Are you aware that military policy includes not only the policy of deterrence, but what is called nuclear war-fighting capabilities, or flexible options? Are you aware of those terms?

A: No, I am not.

Q: Did you ever hear it said by any military officers during your training that such a thing as a nuclear war-fighting capability is something the military is striving for?

A: No.

Q: Could you please tell us what you know about the targeting of Minuteman II missiles?

A: What do you mean by 'targeting'?

Q: Where are they aimed?

A: I don't know. It is not our job to know.

Q: So that although you are responsible for turning the key, you don't know where the missiles are aimed. Is that correct?

A: That is correct.

Q: You have stated that they have a nuclear warhead on top. I understand from published reports that that is a 1.2 megaton nuclear warhead. Would that be correct, to your knowledge?

A: No. It is not correct, to my knowledge.

Q: Do you know the megatonnage of the warhead?

A: I believe 1.2 kilotons.

As later testimony established, Lt. Pollock was mistaken: the yield of the warhead in question is indeed 1.2 megatons, which is one hundred times more powerful than the bomb which destroyed Hiroshima. Pollock had underestimated the power of the weapon by a factor of one thousand.

Q: If a 1.2 kiloton nuclear warhead exploded over Kansas City, do you have any idea of the destruction that would result?

A: I have no idea.

Q: You have no idea. So that although you have been trained to launch these missiles, you don't have very much of an idea what happens when you launch them. Is that correct?

A: I don't know the exact things that would happen. But I turn the key, if I have to, and that is my job.

Present weapons technology—the increased accuracy and yield of modern ICBM's—has rendered all land-based missiles in fixed silos vulnerable to a first-strike attack. Lt. Pollock was apparently unaware of this.

Q: You said that it seems likely that the Minuteman II missile launch facilities are targeted by Soviet missiles. Are they invulnerable to Soviet attack?

A: They are hardened. But I don't really know if they would be vulnerable or invulnerable.

Q: You don't know that. All right. Do you know whether the Minuteman II missile would be usable for retaliation against a Soviet first strike?

A: I have no idea.

Q: You have no idea. In a time of crisis, if these missiles ever have to be launched, do you think there would be time to ask Congress for a declaration of war before the President makes a decision to launch?

U.S. Attorney Stewart: Your Honor, objection.

Judge Hunter: I will let him answer if he knows.

Lt. Pollock: I have no idea.

I think that the issue raised by the tone of Lt. Pollock's responses is not whether or not he is as ignorant as he appears; the issue raised is the fact that there exists in this country a moral climate that permits a person such as Lt. Pollock to be unabashed at the narrowness of his own interpretation of his duty, unabashed at his indifference to the broader implications of his actions.

In addition to Lt. Pollock, the prosecution brought forth several witnesses to describe my arrest, the assessment of the damage to silo N-11, and the details of its repair.

Judge Elmo Hunter seemed to share Lt. Pollock's tendency to see the issues raised by my case in the narrowest possible terms. Before I called my first witness in my defence, the judge felt it necessary to make this statement to the jury:

> I have already explained to the jury that they are a fact-finding jury from the testimony and the evidence in the case. And that they are not

14

concerned with whether or not missile sites are legal or illegal under International Law, or whether the national defence policy is good or bad, effective or ineffective, foolish or not foolish. These are not the issues. Those are large questions of policy, which in the main belong to the President of the United States and to the Congress of the United States; and in any event, they are not an issue in this case. They don't touch the real issues in this case.

My first witness was Dr. Paul Walker, a weapons expert and national security consultant. I was able to question Dr. Walker about the technical characteristics of nuclear weapons systems.

Holladay: Is there any technical reason to say that American nuclear weapons have a first-strike capability?

Dr. Walker: Oh yes. Very definitely. In fact, every weapon we build today is potentially a first-strike weapon... The weapons being deployed today, the Minuteman II amongst them, on both the Soviet and American sides, are driving both sides towards a more hair-trigger reaction. Weapons are being deployed closer to both countries, which means that the launch time is quicker. This weapon takes 30 to 35 minutes to reach the Soviet Union. The new Pershing in Europe takes six minutes. The Soviets have already deployed weapons on submarines off our coast. They take less than six minutes to hit. They are also deploying weapons like Minuteman II, which cannot survive a first-strike attack.

So the only time a Minuteman II can be used is in a first-strike. It is what we call a 'use it or lose it' weapon. It is a real danger, the whole system we have today. A Minuteman II launch crew, whether they know it or not, would be the first to launch nuclear weapons in the world, should they be launched. If they are not the first, they wouldn't launch, because they would be obliterated...

With the increasing accuracy and destructiveness of weapons, with the vulnerability of these silos, the Minuteman II can only be used in an offensive attack, a first-strike attack, against Soviet missiles and military bases. So that the nature of Minuteman has indeed evolved and changed to a much more destablizing, dangerous technology over time.

Q: It would be hard to place the Minuteman II into a deterrence strategy, wouldn't it?

A: Yes. I think that it is impossible today for any land-based missile to be used as a credible second-strike defensive weapon.

Dr. Walker was one of five witnesses I called. I attempted to set forth a defence of justification, which is the principle that an action normally considered a crime is justified, and therefore legal, if it is performed in an attempt to abate an imminent danger. That danger, in this case, is nuclear war. In addition, I tried to refer to numerous treaties and protocols governing the conduct of war, treaties which render nuclear weapons illegal under International Law. The illegitimacy of nuclear weapons would render my disarmament action legal under the Nuremberg principles.

None of my witnesses was allowed to testify freely, since all were subject to some degree of limitation by the court, in response to objections from the prosecutor that the testimony was irrelevant. One of my witnesses, William Durland, who was prepared to testify both to the moral basis for my action and to existing International Law, was not allowed to take the stand at all. I did, however, put myself on the stand to explain my action at the silo.

> The morning of February 19, about dawn, I went to silo N-11, to the Minuteman silo you have seen pictures of, the purpose of which has been described to you – the purpose of which is to launch a missile with a nuclear weapon on it...
>
> There was nobody there at that silo. There are so many silos that they can't man them or guard them. When I got there, it was a quiet morning: a little snow on the ground, very quiet. Right out in the country...
>
> I came to offer an act of disarmament, which is mostly a symbolic act, as you have heard. It involved, literally, the blows of my hammer; but mostly it was a symbolic act. As Dr. Walker explained, I really couldn't do much to make this missile inoperative, because it is so well protected, even against a nuclear attack, short of a direct hit. But I think that it is important that we take steps, concrete action, towards disarmament. They say that the journey of a thousand miles begins with a single step...
>
> Now, damage was done, and we have heard from the maintenance people what that damage was. The damage had to be repaired. The only job of those maintenance people is to repair the damage to make sure that the missile is ready to fire.
>
> But I tell you that it is essential for our very survival that that missile never fire; that that missile not work; that that missile not be launch-ready. If the missile ever launches, we are doomed... We must in fact be sure by whatever means we can bring forth, consistent with non-violence, that that missile never works...
>
> My understanding is that nuclear weapons are illegal under valid, binding laws, international laws which form –

Judge Hunter: Members of the jury, I interrupt again to tell you he is simply saying this to tell you what his state of mind about it is. I have already told you that nuclear weapons *per se* are not illegal under the Constitution and laws of this country.

When all of the evidence and testimony had been presented, the prosecutor had the opportunity to present his closing argument to the jury. In that statement he referred to the fact that my family lived for a time in Beirut, where my father was a missionary during the 1960s.

This is not the Middle East, where we have terrorists that disagree with the government and engage in terrorist actions. That is not the American way of changing policies that you don't like. Mr. Holladay's actions, I suggest, are more akin to those you would expect in Lebanon, where we now find out he grew up – a terrorist-type action...

I am sure that everyone has heard the phrase, 'No man is above the law'. ... That law applies to the judge, it applies to you, and it applies to Mr. Holladay. He violated that law, and it is your duty to find him guilty.

When the prosecutor had finished, I had my own opportunity to address the jury.

You have heard from Mr. Stewart the idea that I might be a terrorist. I ask you to think about your images of terrorism. Did I bring weapons to silo N-11? Did I bring a gun or bomb? Did I flee? Would a terrorist stay there with a piece of paper describing his actions and intent, and sign his name, waiting calmly for arrest? And would a terrorist be standing before you now explaining all of his actions, and be willing to submit to the authority of this court?

Or perhaps the terrorists are someone else: those who now hold every life on earth in hostage; those who aim nuclear weapons that are capable of destroying the entire world. Perhaps *that* is an act of global terrorism? Are we not being held hostage by our own government? Is it not true that every life in this courtroom is threatened this afternoon by nuclear weapons all over the globe? Is there not a pistol to our heads? And who controls that pistol? Who is holding us hostage? Who, then, is the terrorist in this case?

Mr. Stewart has said that none of us is above the law. I ask you if I am acting as if I am above the law: here I am submitting to the law. I am submitting myself to you, the jury, who will come to the verdict in my case. You are the conscience of the community.

But who is holding the nuclear terrorists accountable for their actions? What international body has the power to somehow hold accountable the government who produced these weapons? ... I wish the producers of nuclear weapons could be held accountable. Or is it

17

they who feel that they are above the law—the law that says that every life is sacred, and we cannot be held hostage at their whim?

The judge, in his charge to the jurors, refused to provide instructions which would allow them to consider either of my two main defences, the defence of justification and the International Law defence. After only an hour's deliberation, the jury found me guilty on both charges. One month after the verdict, I was returned to court for sentencing.

> *Judge Hunter*: The message from this court is simply going to be, to everybody who is tempted to do an act similar to yours, that if you do it, be prepared to pay a very substantial penalty. If you intentionally resort to illegal means, expect that the court and judge will not be swayed by words at the time of sentencing, but rather expect that the judge will impose a very substantial sentence...
>
> I sentence you to the custody of the Attorney General of the United States for a period of eight years...
>
> I say this is harsh. It is intended to be harsh... You have simply put yourself as judge and jury in matters that are far beyond your comprehension. You are not in any position to know what proper foreign policy should be at this point.

I am writing these words from the Federal prison in Danbury, Connecticut, where I am serving out my eight-year sentence. The government of course errs in imagining that the people's call for disarmament is successfully repressed by imprisoning resisters: since my sentencing there have been four more Plowshares actions. Thirty-one Plowshares activists are now in prison in the USA, serving sentences ranging from one to eighteen years.

The choice between the power of force and the power of non-violence grows more polarized each year, as the technology of our weaponry becomes more absolute, and as the consistent choice of love seems to require an ever-broader leap of faith. We are all burdened with a collection of fears that render us reluctant to make that leap. Meanwhile the policy-makers who justify war are preparing for a future far more terrifying than any that can be conjured up by our fears of the consequences of loving our enemies. The apparent bleakness of the choice of remaining armed paradoxically helps to kindle our hope: our hope in a growing community that chooses disarmament, which is our only alternative.

---

*Quotations from courtroom proceedings come from the official court transcript of the trial.

18

CHAPTER TWO

Why Me? Why Not?

TODD KAPLAN

Todd Kaplan, 30, was sentenced to three years in an American prison for his part in one of the 'Plowshares' actions in which he, and seven others, used hammers to damage Pershing II ballistic missiles being manufactured in an aerospace plant in Florida. In the past he has worked among the poor in Washington DC to provide for them the essentials of life. As a Jew he has spent a year in Israel, with Arabs, Christians and Jews, at the community of Neve Shalom, attempting to bring about reconciliation between those conflicting factions. During this period he also tried, with a small group of other Jews, to trace Palestinian prisoners of the war, captured by Israeli forces in Lebanon.

In this article, written in prison, he describes vividly how contact with other peace activists in the United States convinced him that he too had to make a very personal commitment to disarmament — to carry out what he regards as an act of 'holocaust prevention'.

He was released from prison in July 1986, having served twenty-seven months of his sentence.

Over the last two years while I've been in prison serving time for my participation in a Plowshares disarmament action, I have attempted at various times to reach out beyond the prison to describe what moved me to join this struggle in this way. Each time that I've set pen to paper, I've come around to thinking about those individuals that I met and worked with, these same individuals that have eventually ended up participating in a Plowshares action themselves. In many ways, knowing them has encouraged me and helped me move from a passive role to a more active one, from a sense that I needed to work for social justice through direct service to the poor to an understanding that bringing peace and non-violence to the world is the same task as feeding and sheltering the poor and homeless.

Knowing these people, seeing them act — risking their liberty and then doing the jail time — made me look at myself and question my commitment to peace...what was holding me back from taking a more active role? I recognized the moral significance of the Plowshares. I could see the clarity of the 'no' to the means of mass suicide and the 'yes' to supporting life. But certainly I did not see myself willing or able to sacrifice my liberty (and possibly more)... for anything. For a few years I dwelled on the subject, discounting the value of the time spent in prison, the 'jail witness'; convincing myself that I was not made of the same heroics and courage that these 'Plowshares' people were made of until, through knowing the few that I came into contact with, I began to see that they were no more clear-headed, courageous or strong than me (or you?). But they *had* travelled that road that leads to taking more responsibility in a time that demands much of each of us. I would like to be able to take you by the hand and introduce you to each of these people so that you too could see that these down-to-earth people are just doing what is necessary and demanded of us for our times. Of course I can't do that, but perhaps across these pages, across time and distance, I can introduce you to a few of the people who have touched me and my work. Perhaps I can share with you a little of the journey that led me to the Plowshares campaign.

My first contact with the Plowshares came about when a few of us from the soup-kitchen staff in Washington DC hopped in the van early one morning to travel to the site of the first trial for a Plowshares action; the trial of the Plowshares Eight. When we arrived, it was raining and cold and the courtroom was already full of spectators. I had only one glove as we joined a few others and held a vigil outside the courthouse in Norristown, a small town in Pennsylvania and the nearest court to the General Electric weapons plant that manufactured the MX missile. Inside, the Plowshares Eight were on trial for an action that had startled me and many of my friends in the peace and justice movement.

I had only heard the names of those involved and I would not meet any of them personally for at least a couple more years. But, as I huddled holding that banner on the courthouse steps, all I could think of was how brave and prophetic these people were. I was moved and challenged by what they had done: walking into a high security area of the plant, taking hammers and bottles of blood out of their attaché cases and working on the MX missile nose-cones (turning them into scrap metal) ...but surely I would never do anything like this. This wasn't for me?

This was different. The Plowshares Eight had crossed the line from the vigil and simple trespass — a line that had marked protests for disarmament to that time — to a form of action that struck a different note, a note of urgency. This act was like a shout for help by a victim in a crowded city — the type of shout that usually goes ignored — but this cry of moral outrage at the first-strike MX pierced the souls of all who dared to listen. It was truly disruptive of the status quo, and as such carried a much greater risk of punishment. This shook me.

I thought about the various acts of civil disobedience that I had participated in. In each case I had just stood there, or crossed a line demonstrating my convictions in a public and sometimes orchestrated manner. Another significant difference was that each participant in the Plowshares Eight was offering up his or her liberty in a more than symbolic way (they were risking years in prison, not months or days) as a means of addressing an evil of pressing importance — our acceptance of nuclear weapons as a means of resolving international conflict.

The symbols of the action shone brightly even through the dense fog of media interpretations. The creation of the 'community of conscience', the step into the moral abyss, and the embodiment of the biblical mandate (from Isaiah) — the hammer forging the sword into a 'plowshare' — all these things spoke of a new path. It is a path that points both to the end — a disarmed world void of violence and injustice — and the means of reaching this goal: through non-violent struggle and self-sacrifice. I recall Sister Anne Montgomery (a participant in the Plowshares Eight and two other Plowshares since), who spoke of picking up her hammer and bringing it down on the missile cone. Hearing the loud ring, she looked to see if a dent was there — the first act of dulling the sword... the initiation of disarmament.

Later after her third Plowshare, the 'Pershing Plowshares', she wrote from Florida:

...When we beat a sword (be it Trident, Mark 12A, Cruise or Pershing) into a plowshare, the plowshare, seemingly unshaped, is the community being formed: in our case a little community of eight forging new bonds with a growing community in Florida and beyond (especially in Per Herngren's Sweden!) This particular power of truth/love force became evident that Easter dawn as we were left in our praying and singing circle while police and employees explored our 'workshop'. Instead of becoming angrier (and we had feared their guns), they seemed touched by something of the non-violent spirit of that day and moment, interrupting us only at breaks between prayers and treating us with a kind of respect.

There have, of course, been other reactions. As we work through our hearings, the judge attempts to build a wall of legal language and misinterpretation around us, calling everything we say and write a non-defence of 'motive': our intent to defend life; the necessity which determined our manner of action; our obedience to the Constitution and International Law, to say nothing of the Law of God. But language imprisons him, not us, nor does it imprison those willing to walk through the walls of fear — trusting that inner as well as outer doors will open — to experience the meaning of truth and love, in however small a way, and be humble before an experience for which words are difficult and inadequate. The one that keeps bubbling up into my consciousness is 'vulnerability': a shared experience on both sides of the fences and courtroom benches. When we can learn to accept it as a gift rather than an evil or weakness, we will be able to actualize more and more symbolic, but real, beating of swords into plowshares.'

As an observer of the movement, I was deeply affected by the spirit of hope that came forth from the trial of the Plowshares Eight. Songs were sung (and written), a festival of hope was celebrated, and a community of support emerged. The actions of the judge and prosecutor only served to highlight the spring of hope that flowed forth from the eight defendants. As I left the trial behind, returning to my home and work in Washington, I was both impressed and confused. I was not entirely convinced of the value of these obviously religious individuals giving up years of their lives in prisons. I wondered, what does it mean to the world and to God, to have these activists taken from us—locked away? I wondered about the appropriateness of the action. Was it an act of courage or desperation? Was it prophetic or heretical? Only over time would I come up with some answers to these questions.

I continued to work in Washington DC with a small group of men and women (the Community for Creative Non-Violence/CCNV) who were working to provide food and housing for the homeless. There I was able to lose myself in the work, as it was very demanding. I rose each day to the challenge of gathering together the wherewithal to feed hundreds (often five hundred) of Washington's poor. A key aspect of this group's work that later helped me to connect with my future role in the Plowshares movement was that as providers of service to the poor, we also knocked on the doors of the Church and State, reminding them of the homeless, those who have no voice and won't just 'go away'. 'Knocking on the door' was our euphemism for the peaceful, non-violent sit-ins and protests that organically grew out of the work. For example when there was no room in the existing shelters for all of the homeless, we opened a shelter (through occupying it) in a wing of the weatherproof and heated but unused train station. This particular action led to the creation of hundreds of additional beds for the homeless at other more suitable locations.

Our use of direct intervention naturally led us to associate with many peace groups that saw that their struggle for peace and disarmament was the same as ours for social justice. I, too, came to understand that our struggle was the same. I realized that the same values that allow us as a society to ignore the plight of the homeless also allow us to contemplate and prepare for the ending of all life through a runaway arms race. Even when we articulate different values − for example that life is 'sacred' − this is not borne out by our actions. I began to see how this small group (CCNV), with its service to the poor and appeals to the public conscience, was part of the same effort as the peace/disarmament movement. Both were attempting to build from the ground up a world that wouldn't and couldn't depend on nuclear weapons as a means of solving conflict and would see service to the poor not as the gift of charity but as the upholding of righteousness. As I began to meet people who later took part in a Plowshares disarmament action, gradually through these relationships I began to realize that I too could (and should) participate in a Plowshares action.

So, let me introduce you to Helen Woodson, Carl Kabat, Paul Magno, Marcia Timmel, Roger Ludwig, John LaForge, Barb Katt, and Jean Holladay: a few of those who have encouraged me by their actions and lives so that I too was able to take up the banner of the Plowshares and carry it forward and perhaps pass it on to you.

Helen Woodson is often looked upon as a stubborn and uncompromising woman, but I look to her as an anchor of principle unwilling to bend with each gust of wind. Helen has worked for years as a caring

mother looking after her own 'home-grown' son and several adopted
and handicapped foster children as well. Like most of us she remained
distanced from peace activities, until relatively recently. At her trial in
Kansas City, Missouri for her part in the Silo Pruning Hooks protest,
she told the jury:

> I can only speak the truth with my life, that above all else, we
> owe our children a safe and peaceful world.

Long before she spoke these words, Helen put them into practice, first
working in a supportive role, editing and publishing a chronicle of the
activist side of the peace movement entitled 'Harvest of Justice'. Over
the next few years she chose her acts of conscience carefully, always
making sure that her children were well cared for with baby-sitters.
Each act was a clearer statement of her rejection of violence and also
entailing a greater risk of imprisonment. One act that I remember (and
for which she received a six-month sentence in the Washington DC jail)
was when she poured blood on a missile on display at the Air and Space
museum on Hiroshima Day.

Helen tells of her journey to act in a Plowshares action in her
summation to the jury:

> You have heard mention of children here, and children have been
> much on my mind, since I have not seen mine for three months.
> I'd have to say that my resistance began twenty years ago with a
> child. It was 1964 and I was taking my son to meet his grandparents
> for the first time. The train was crowded, mostly with servicemen on
> Christmas leave. We pulled into the Pittsburg station late at night and
> the snow and ice and condensation fogging the windows. We sat and sat
> in the station until someone wondered why we weren't moving and wiped
> the windows. Outside was an honor guard watching as the caskets from
> Vietnam were unloaded. The Pittsburg boys come home for Christmas.
>
> I held my son, my infant, and whispered what every mother of sons
> has said in every bloody generation all over the world, 'Never you'. And
> then I went home and did what every mother has done in every bloody
> generation all over the world. I did nothing. Through some miracle, my
> son has lived to grow up and is here in the courtroom today. Now Selec-
> tive Service wants him to register for the draft so that he too can some
> day come home for Christmas in a box. I can no longer do nothing.

She then challenged the jury to consider the facts of the case in
the light of the nuclear age:

> So now you come to deliberate. I'll make it easy for you. We are guilty.
> We are guilty of acting to leave human life where it properly belongs –

in the hands of the Lord who created it. We are guilty of proclaiming with our act that the Law of God supersedes the law of the US, Thou shall not kill! We are guilty of declaring with our act the supremacy of faith, morality and conscience over systems and rules. We are guilty of rendering unto Caesar exactly what Caesar deserves — absolutely nothing — and unto God what rightly belongs to God — absolutely everything. Of loving life, of loving God and his Law, of loving truth and human conscience — of all that, we are guilty.

It did not take long before the jury, following the judge's lead, found them guilty. The judge sentenced Helen Woodson and Carl Kabat, Paul Kabat and Larry Cloud Morgan to the harshest sentences for a Plowshares protest to date: 18, 18, 10 and 8 years respectively.

Helen is now a resident of the Federal Women's Prison in Alderson, West Virginia, thousands of miles from her children, who are taken care of by full-time baby-sitters. Her eighteen-year sentence has now been unilaterally reduced by the judge to twelve years and several years of probation.

It is sad to contemplate that such a wonderful person as Helen will be spending this lengthy period in prison. Helen asks that we do not focus on gaining her release or shortening her sentence, but that we channel our time, energy, and resources towards eliminating the violence represented by nuclear weapons. In this way Helen's sacrifice will serve to focus our attention where it rightly belongs; on that capacity for evil within us that passively accepts nuclear weapons.

Father Carl Kabat is one quarter of the Silo Pruning Hooks group and is now serving his prison term in Milan, Michigan. I've known him for years, first from a distance when I saw him as a defendant in the Plowshares Eight trial; later I became closer to him when I joined him and many others at vigils at the Pentagon. Carl is one of those people who seems to be always there: holding a banner, singing a song, or chanting a chant with a seriousness and friendliness that says we must be about our work, but let's not lose our sense of humor! Carl worked with the poor in Brazil and returned to the USA awakened to our collective and individual responsibility for both world poverty and the runaway arms race. In his statement of conscience that he left at the silo he wrote:

> Over 50 years of age, 25 of priesthood, missionary work in the Philippines and South America, and the Gospels have taught me that personal responsibility for everything done in our name is a requirement for anyone attempting to be a Christian.

As citizens of God's kingdom on earth, we are called to stand against, with our bodies and souls, the usurpation of God's prerogatives on earth. At one time only God could destroy the earth, but now we creatures can destroy it and all life many times over. We offer our pinch of incense to Caesar by our taxes, by our refusal to do clear public actions against the idolatry of nuclear annihilation and the starving of our brothers and sisters.

Our country's carpet-bombing of Dresden and the nuclear destruction of Hiroshima and Nagasaki have prepared us to accept the preparation for mass murder done in our name. Like the German people who accepted the legality of the holocaust, we by our lack of continuous clear public actions accept the possibility of the final idolatry.

I am celebrating my silver anniversary of the priesthood by beginning the disarmament of one missile silo; I invite you to do the same with the other 1048. 'Choose life that you and your children may live' by breaking the laws that protect the nuclear idols of our time.

No one can say that Carl didn't know what he was getting into — this was his third Plowshare. It is clear that as he endures his time in prison, his presence is a reminder that our work is not done.

Of several couples involved in resistance that I've met and worked with, I have known Marcia Timmel and Paul Magno best. They have managed to integrate work for justice and peace into their lives. The two branches of their efforts are direct service to the homeless in Washington DC and resistance to the terror of nuclear weapons. I first got to know them well as I helped them rehabilitate a terraced house in inner-city Washington. This became their home that they shared with the poorest of the poor — America's homeless.

As they first worked with homeless men and later moved on to the Dorothy Day Hospitality House for families (mostly women and children) this work seemed totally engrossing. It was and continues to be extremely valuable work that deals with' the real and pressing needs of families for comfort, food, clothing, and shelter. This house where Marcia and Paul now serve houses nearly twenty-five women and children.

When I joined the staff at the house prior to acting in the Pershing Plowshares in the Spring of 1984, I noticed that all staff developed a sense of personal obligation to the guests to help them get back on their own in a stable living situation. When Paul and I initially thought of being part of a Plowshares we had to weigh the essentially abstract nature of our symbolic bringing of hammer to 'sword' against the real demands and needs of the homeless who shared our home.

By their actions — both have participated in Plowshares actions — it is clear that Paul and Marcia have both decided that the risk of nuclear war and the danger that it presents to those families that they struggle to protest and provide shelter for is so great that they must also address these dangers.

This of course has not come about without fear, stress, or the tearing of the fabric of their relationship to each other and their work with the homeless. But they *have* held together, and when one or the other has been absent — vigilling, participating in non-violent resistance, or serving time in prison — others have come forward to keep the necessary services for the homeless going.

Another element of Paul and Marcia's marriage that has been set aside is their wish to have children. I remember suggesting to Paul as we initially faced forty-year sentences (between Federal and State charges — later mostly dropped) that he make the most of his pre-trial freedom! As it turned out though, Paul and Marcia's faith that a time for children will present itself has been fulfilled, as Paul was released in February of 1986 and they are expecting their first child in December.

This commitment to justice and peace that is bound up in the essence of their marriage is an example for me. They and a few others, most notably the durable marriage of Phil Berrigan and Elizabeth McAlister, have shown me that a life of service to the poor, resistance to violence, the building of community, and also maintaining a stable relationship and marriage are not impossible goals. They have also shown me that these commitments do not make for an easy life, but are certainly worth the effort to achieve. I see that I need not forgo relationships and marriage in order to give of myself in a Plowshares campaign; indeed relationships, marriage, and community may give me the strength to continue to act in accordance with my conscience in the future.

Pilgrim Song

The least I can do,
The most I can do,
Is wait for you,
Is wait with you,
Alone, not alone
For the coming liberation
That never comes,
That may never come,

27

That comes ever
In our waiting.

The least I can do,
The most I can do
Is greet you on the way
To where we know not,
To one who knows not,
And knows.

Roger Ludwig

Roger Ludwig is a quiet, religious, sensitive man who is both a poet and a fine pianist. He is also someone who has spent a considerable amount of time performing the simple tasks — such as mopping the floors — that are required to run a shelter for the homeless. We worked together at the shelter and soup-kitchens of Washington DC and saw many a broken soul; all who were intoxicated and sick, unemployed and lonely — all who were deemed disposable by society. Roger saw — long before I did — the need for non-violent protest against the arms race at the Pentagon, the White House, and the weapons plants and bases — the bastions of power that celebrate the means of faster, more efficient death. As he stepped back from his work at the shelters to take part in a Plowshare, I wondered at this strength that permitted him to jump into a risk that entails prison sentences of unknown lengths. When would he resume his chores at the infirmary for the homeless where he had last lived and worked? How well would he deal with prison? I was frightened for him, and for myself too as his step forward challenged me to do the same. I was filled with fear of the unknown.

I met Barb Katt and John LaForge in Washington DC. They had come from Bemiji, Minnesota in the northern, rural mid-west to join the same series of protests that had brought Jean Holladay to Washington in 1981. They reminded me a little of young pioneers of days past, venturing to the big city. They were a little taken aback by the legions of media and the grand production that our protests often resembled. This was all somewhat different from Bemiji, the small college town where they had studied and protested, where they were somewhat the conscience of the community. They now live on a farm, and I'm sure that the natural beauty, tranquillity and security of the area leaves little to be desired. But in August of 1984 they set all of this aside and set out one morning dressed as quality control inspectors and entered a Sperry weapons plant in Minneapolis.

Unlikely Q.C. inspectors though they were, this didn't get them stopped when they entered an area where prototype computers for the Trident were being built. The true intent of their business was soon revealed as hammers came out, blood was poured, and indictments for war crimes were passed out to representatives of the company. They were tried (and convicted) in a 'quick two-day affair' as John wrote me, 'with the two of us standing alone against the law'. At sentencing, John and Barb both spoke of their decision to deal with a future made insecure by nuclear weapons — a predicament we all face. In John's words:

> With acceptance, silence and complicity we have lived and live today alongside steady preparations for nuclear holocaust. The Chinese tell us, 'If we do not change our direction, we're likely to end up where we're headed.' But like a person dying for many days, we are numb to the stench. Sperry's plans, our plans, for weapons of mass extermination — like the Trident and F-4G, part of which we disarmed — are utterly and absolutely horrible.
>
> We all know that hydrogen bombs cannot be used with either military practicality or ethical justification. We've banned not only the wanton burning of innocent people, but the planning of such an act. In human terms, then, nuclear weapons are useless and blasphemous and absurd. Building more, like the misuse of drugs or alcohol, is a form of chronic suicide.
>
> The insanity doesn't end here. The US alone has ominously created 290,000 cubic meters of high-level radioactive waste from the making of bombs that serve no purpose. Cancers of all kinds proliferate among our children, ourselves and our parents. 'Continue to contaminate your bed,' warned Chief Seattle 150 years ago, 'and you will one night suffocate in your waste.'
>
> Individually, we can do very little to keep this from happening.
>
> Most people admit to the possibility of such a war, but the belief that disarmament can happen is almost unheard of.

Later on he described the disarmament itself:

> We were nearly unable to overcome our fear of failure in our disarmament act. I may never have believed truly that it was possible to succeed, only that it was right to try; that attempt was and still is universally correct.
>
> No matter what happens now, the action will always be invaluable to me. It convinced me that the arms race can be halted non-violently. It is possible to arrest the forward momentum, because the two of us with the help of our friends delayed for months the delivery of prototype nuclear weapons parts.

Barb, who made only one demand of the judge at sentencing — that she and John be given the same sentence — commented that:

> Most of us build prisons for ourselves and after we occupy them for a period of time we become accustomed to their walls and accept the false premise that we are incarcerated for life. As soon as that belief takes hold of us we abandon hope of ever doing more with our lives and of ever giving our dreams a chance to be fulfilled. We begin to suffer living deaths; one of a herd heading for destruction in a grey mass of mediocrity.
>
> In our act of disarmament, in all its preparations and what has come since, I have found a lifeline of hope, the resurrection of hope from a living death. I resist not only the nuclear arms race, but the spiritual darkness of futility and self-pity as well. Hope is alive in the courtroom today.

These statements and the straightforward personal testimony that Barb and John presented must have pierced the wall of the law. Certainly it is obvious from the judge's remarks that they must have touched a resonating chord of dissent in the judge that was released at their sentencing:

> As I ponder over the punishment to be meted out to these two people who were attempting to unbuild weapons of mass destruction, we must ask ourselves: Can it be that those of us who build weapons to kill are engaged in a more sanctified endeavor than those who would by their acts attempt to counsel moderation and mediation as an alternative method of settling international disputes... How can we even entertain the thought that all people on one side of an imaginary line must die and, if we be so ungodly cynical as to countenance that thought, have we given thought to the fact that in executing that decree we will also die...
>
> How many people in this democracy have seriously contemplated the futility of committing national suicide in order to punish our adversaries. Have we so little faith in our system of free enterprise, our capitalism and the fundamental constitutions and in our several bibles that we must, in order to protect ourselves from the spread of foreign ideologies, be prepared to die at our own hands. Such thinking indicates a great lack of faith in our democracy, our body politic, our people, and our institutions...
>
> The inexorable pressure which generates from those who are engaged in making a living and a profit from building military equipment and the pork barrelling that goes on in the halls of Congress to obtain more such contracts for the individual state will ultimately consume itself in an atomic holocaust. These same factors exert a powerful pressure upon a judge in my position to go along with the theory that there is something sacred about a bomb and that those who raise their voices or their hands against it should be struck down as enemies of the people, no matter that in their hearts they feel and know that they are friends of the people.

Now conduct of this sort cannot be condoned under the guise of free speech. Neither should it be totally condemned as being subversive, traitorous, or treasonous in the category of espionage. I would here in this instance take the sting out of the bomb, attempt in some way to force the government to remove the halo with which it seems to embrace any device which can kill and to place thereon a shroud, the shroud of death, destruction, mutilation, disease and debilitation.

If there be an adverse reaction to this sentence, I will anxiously await the protestations of those who complain of my attempts to correct the imbalance that now exists in a system that operates in such a manner as to provide one type of justice for the rich and a lesser type for the poor. One standard for the mighty and another for the meek. And a system which finds its humanness and objectivity is sublimated to military madness and the worship of the bomb.

And with these and a few other comments he then proceeded to sentence John and Barb to a six-month suspended sentence and six months' probation, a tap on the wrist compared with the potential five-year sentence.

I met Jean Holladay when she came to join us in 1981 in Washington for a month to support a month-long vigil/protest and civil disobedience at the White House in the beginning of the Reagan administration. Jean was a powerhouse of endurance and strength and she mixed easily with the hundreds of peace and justice activists that came out to 'vote' with their bodies. She was always there where she was needed; stirring the soup-kitchen pot or assisting with the various service projects for the homeless that we continued to run. She was also quick to volunteer to participate in the civil disobedience or assist those for whom this was all too new.

As I heard of her participation in one Plowshares after another, first in November of 1982 and then again in July of 1983, I was reminded of her glowing spirit and natural warmth. I don't think that I ever saw her shout or get angry or hesitate to lend a hand. She really is a natural leader, not because you see her pounding the podiums or shouting rhetoric, but because of her example. She has now participated in three Plowshares, each time risking lengthy periods in prison. Perhaps what drives her is a vision of what it takes to build a world without nuclear weapons. She writes (with Art Laffin, another Plowshares activist):

If nuclear disarmament is to be a reality in our time, it will not happen merely by political decrees. It will occur because people want peace with such a passion that risks are gladly accepted. While actions each person chooses to take for peace may vary, the moral responsibility to resist the

31

unprecedented nuclear peril exists for us all — to resist in such a way that our whole lives become means of transformation and healing.

Following her example in February 1985, her son Martin initiated Plowshares 'Number 12' for which he was sentenced to eight years, which he is now serving in a Federal Prison in Danbury, Connecticut.

Jean has now finished the one-year prison sentence for her participation in her third Plowshare, the 'Trident 2' Plowshares. Jean, whose primary mission has always been to serve life, plans to take care of her grandchildren. The children's mother, her daughter, was recently killed by a hit-and-run driver.

> Some look to the Holocaust and Hiroshima and Nagasaki and see this as the warning of times to come. I wonder is this the final test of faith, if we acquiesce to the extermination of all, north and south, east and west — what will we be? We will have failed and we will have put up all of humanity on the altar of greed, ignorance and the shunning away from faith.
>
> *Larry Cloud Morgan*

'What will we be if we do not act?' The Plowshares have chosen to address this question head-on. From these glimpses of just a few of the Plowshares activists, you can see that we have varied backgrounds and careers, but we have all united in our dissent and hope. Dissenting openly and forcefully proclaiming that the suicide/genocide pact that exists by our silent consent must be broken. Hope that our acts will be seen by God and the citizens of the world as acts of love taken in the defence of life. Hope that together we can hold back the darkness of pessimism and doom. Hope that we can recreate a world in the mould of peace and justice.

But how many have we reached? What good have we done by our sacrifice of liberty? Has our strategy been effective? To respond to these questions let me share with you the answers of Helen Woodson, Elizabeth McAlister, Clare Grady, Jackie Allen, and Sister Anne Montgomery as they were interviewed by another political activist and fellow inmate, Shelley Miller, at the Federal Women's Prison in Alderson, West Virginia.

Question: What is the goal of your actions? What strategy or vision do they reflect?

Clare: In our action, we tried to embody a vision, not necessarily a game plan or a structure. We're trying to live out relationships in community as contrasted with relationships to the state and property. In hammering on the object, you are making clear your relationship to that object in unequivocal terms. But it's controlled, without threat to human life. We're also saying that while we are responsible for bombs and disarmament, disarmament will not come about solely through our efforts or by force − that would be the same kind of violence. Disarmament starts with the inner person.

Liz: The most appealing of several visions to me is one of disarming − what it actually looks like, and how we get there. The weapons express us as a people and a nation. There's something in us that the weapons fulfil. We must change our relationship to them. Disarming a particular weapon is a symbol of a broader and deeper disarmament of the spirit. Entering into a disarming action means trying to live in a disarmed way − vulnerable and open.

Anne: I think the fundamental change is deeper than getting rid of weapons systems. Fundamental change must come in terms of change in ourselves and in our perceptions of power and violence. Violence is exported along with weapons. Look at Nicaragua and El Salavador. So how we communicate our non-violence and need for a change of heart is much more important than how we disarm a particular weapon. I don't particularly hope to change large groups of people. Change comes from small groups, small communities. I think in terms of in-depth change in a few, rather than many going out to demonstrate and then returning to ordinary life. People on the fringe begin to pull the main body along. The few begin to shift the focus of the others.

Jackie: I don't believe in strategy and all that. We don't need just to disarm weapons, because actually *people* make weapons. And you can't disarm people with a hammer. I think of the Buddhist saying 'Embrace the tasks, relinquish the fruits of the labor'. It's not for me to know the end results of my action. If I choose to do good, particularly in relationship with other people and the cosmos, the result has to be better than not doing good. I come at non-violence from a spiritual point of view. Spiritual death is worse than physical death, and if I used violence, the result for me would be spiritual death.

Helen: I don't think in terms of strategy at all, but in terms of acceptance of personal responsibility and obedience to the Gospel. First and foremost, a speaking of the truth that stems from moral/spiritual principles: (1) total commitment to non-violence. That means no threat of physical harm to others and an invitation into reconciliation, freedom and community; (2) acceptance of the consequences of one's actions and a willingness to endure suffering rather than inflict it; (3) the spiritual dimension of action (Judeo-Christian, Native American, earth-centered) which places emphasis on hope and faith rather than immediate effectiveness.

Question: But how *do* you see the effectiveness of your actions, the building of them — whom have they affected?

Helen: My goal was not to change others, because I don't know how that's done. I kind of believe the transformation of the human heart is God's province. My responsibility was to do what I could in relationship to that one weapon. I hope that the truth we tried to express can be communicated in a way that touches others, but ultimately we are responsible only for our own actions, not other's reactions.

Liz: Disarmament will occur when there is a clear public will to disarm. Then the leadership will have to disarm. I think our actions are one beginning voice, small at this time, saying disarmament is absolutely necessary. But disarmament will be costly. We can't continue to live as we have. The whole economic structure must change. Jobs and wealth are geared to the arms race. We're saying some are willing to risk life, freedom, relationships. I hope for change in people's lives but it's not our job to say what will be. This is part of the gift you hope for in acting.

Beyond these words there is little more to add. We pray that we will be part of the beginnings of the movement to build a world void of nuclear weapons, a world where the value of life would be supreme. We may not know if in our lifetimes our actions will be the key to that necessary change. In fact we do not claim to have all the answers. We can only claim that we are struggling to respond in a non-violent manner to some critical questions. We make no attempt to quantify or analyse the numbers of 'converts' to our cause, but we do see movement. We find hope in the groundswell of grassroots resistance here and abroad that is now evident.

This is the kind of change — that which is integrated into our lives — that we seek. This is the necessary change: the restructuring of our relationships both between each other and between nations. With this prayer and vision, we hope that we all take a share of the work, and move forward both in and out of prisons together.

CHAPTER THREE

Why I went to Greenham

SIAN CHARNLEY

Sian Charnley, a language graduate of Bristol University, was born in Wales but has spent most of her life in England. Before her marriage she was a teacher in a comprehensive school in London. Now, as a mother of three young children, she divides her energies between caring for her children's immediate needs and working for a world in which they can grow up free of the fear of nuclear war. She has been arrested six times for her non-violent demonstrations against the deployment of nuclear weapons in the UK, and has been imprisoned on three occasions.

When the first flight of Cruise missiles eventually arrived in Greenham Common in November 1983, my despair was deep and personal. I remember waiting at the school gates for my children and feeling utterly alone, because nobody else seemed to be aware of what was happening. Yet all over the country, I am sure, other mothers of young children must have been feeling the same as I did. One of the reasons I am writing this is that my awakening awareness of, and involvement with, the peace movement, so closely linked as it was to the bringing up of small children, must have paralleled that of many other people.

The emphasis on prison is not one I would have chosen, because going to prison was almost incidental to my involvement with the peace movement. But the fact that I had already had two short stays in prison before Cruise arrived could be seen as symbolic of the disruption that struggling for peace was bringing to my family life. It was certainly the aspect of my work most 'visible' to other people. The real disruption came from evening after evening of meetings, at the time in our lives when sleep was already disturbed by small children, days spent planning or going to demonstrations, and the many and varied campaigning activities, with which anyone connected with CND will be familiar.

Before having children, I had had very little involvement with politics. My upbringing was conventional and uneventful. My schoolteacher parents moved from Mid-Wales to Southampton when I was seven, and there I later attended a Direct Grant girls' school, where nobody was encouraged to question anything. Apart from turning out regularly to vote Labour at general elections, my parents showed no great interest in politics. I drifted into University to do a language degree, because it seemed to follow on naturally from what I'd done before. There, for the first time, because of the people I met, rather than anything I studied, I began to question the way we live. Between 1967 and 1970, the years during which I was at Bristol University, the 'hippy' movement popularised for people of my age the idea of impending ecological disaster if industrial society continued on its present course. It never occurred to me, however, that I could actually change anything in society, even though I gradually made changes in my own life-style. The anti-Vietnam war movement seemed remote and too vast to comprehend.

During the early 1970s I was very busy being a teacher in demanding London comprehensive schools, and in forming a relationship with Norman, my husband-to-be. I developed my interest in environmental and ecological subjects by reading, and during the mid-seventies, horrified by what I read on the subject, I went on marches and rallies against nuclear power. Nuclear weapons and nuclear war were things I'd always pushed to the back of my mind. I remember being a child of twelve during the Cuba Crisis, when it seemed to me that I might die of fright. I was only too happy to seize upon and accept the adult explanations of the 'deterrence' theory and reassurance that it would work; even though I was uneasily aware that the grown-ups too showed terror in their eyes. Now when I read books about nuclear power, I skipped the chapters explaining the links with nuclear weapons, because I found the whole subject too painful to face.

My marriage and my children have been the most important things in my life. My first daughter, Maggie, was born in Cambridge in 1977, and my second daughter, Anna, was born in Oxford in 1979. At a time when I was sharing my children's growing awareness of the richness, diversity and beauty of the world, and at a time when my personal future had never seemed brighter, it was announced in the December of the year of Anna's birth that this country would accept American Cruise missiles. At this point it was believed that some would be stationed at Upper Heyford, ten miles from Oxford: ten miles from my children.

Soon afterwards the Russians invaded Afghanistan and we were reminded that the unthinkable, a third world war in our lifetime, was possible. In March 1981 I watched a television programme about the government's civil defence plans for a nuclear war. These plans, as contained in the government leaflet *Protect and Survive*, were so painfully inadequate as to appear callous. I could no longer go and look at the faces of my sleeping children without feeling a deep and almost numbing sense of despair. I could no longer bear to make plans for their future.

My husband helped me. He bought me a copy of E.P. Thompson's *Protest and Survive*, which, although it catalogued even more reasons for being afraid, stressed the need for positive action. 1983 was a deadline; if Cruise missiles arrived it would be too late. Together we decided to be active. At first I sat in Campaign ATOM (Oxford CND) meetings feeling overawed by the seeming expertise of the other participants. But by the end of the year I had been on demonstrations, written letters, and become involved in setting up a campaigning group in a small local area of Oxford of about half a dozen streets. I had helped to organise a meeting of parents in Maggie's pre-school playgroup. Naively I had thought that one had only to alert parents to the nuclear threat and that they would all become active overnight.

During 1981 and 1982 the little spare time that I had was increasingly absorbed by local campaigning, such as collecting signatures on petitions, showing films, and holding public meetings. In March 1982, the day after a life-affirming festival at Greenham Common, I took part in a twenty-four hour blockade of the base. I was not yet prepared to break the law myself, but I had the role of 'legal observer' at one of the gates. Already it was apparent to me that the so-called democratic process was letting us down in our struggle. Members of Parliament were uninformed and seemed disinclined to inform themselves. Parliament gave little priority to an issue which would affect life on this planet for ever. The whole nuclear industry had a history of secrecy and lies. The media either ignored the issue or misrepresented peace campaigners. I knew that the women sitting in the mud at Greenham and refusing to let lorries through were right. Nobody else was taking responsibility; they would take it themselves. If that base were to continue to function normally for the next twenty-four hours, then it would happen only by removing their bodies.

The might of people engaged in non-violent direct action such as this was conveyed to others. Despair was turning into hope. Some women convicted after this blockade and similar actions refused to accept their convictions for breach of the peace and were sent to prison. I'm sure that this helped to swell the numbers of women (more than 30,000) who arrived to 'Embrace the Base' at Greenham on December 12, 1982.

Earlier that year, in April, a peace camp was established at Upper Heyford. Although Heyford was no longer a proposed site for Cruise missiles, it was and is one of the most operational nuclear bases in Europe, and as such needed to be 'put on the map'. To me at that time, peace camps seemed to have an important role to play. Where the death-camps, the nuclear bases, stood on the landscape making a symbolic statement, an opposing, more hopeful statement could be made by a group of people living peaceably next to it. Nobody could ignore these bases any more. Soon nobody would be able to say, as someone whom I was canvassing in Oxford not long before had said, 'Nuclear weapons at Upper Heyford, love? No. They're having you on.'

It was important to me, then, that this little peace camp should survive. After it was set up and until it was very firmly established, I would try to stay there one night a week, sometimes longer, often with two-year-old Anna. It was something that I could do that was compatible with looking after children, and this too was important. Anna loved camping, and I am sure from things she has said since that some of the optimism and wisdom of the people who lived there permanently at that time permeated her limited understanding of the world.

On 31 December 1982 there was a short blockade of the base at Upper Heyford. This time I went prepared if necessary to be arrested.

But the authorities chose to close the base for the day rather than risk peaceful confrontation with the blockade.

By now, public awareness of Cruise missiles was growing; Upper Heyford and developments there were equally ominous, and I decided to give my personal priority to acivities there for the time being. While the public seemed relatively receptive to new knowledge about nuclear weapons, it was important that they should be made aware too of as many parts of the obscene jigsaw as possible. Cruise missiles were only one tip of the iceberg.

It was planned to extend the base at Upper Heyford to build hangars to house EF-111 planes. These, with their electronic radar-jamming equipment, flying in conjunction with the F-111 planes already there, would render the F-111s invisible to 'enemy' radar, and thus make them potential 'first-strike weapons'. We knew that the building of this extension would start some time early in 1983, and from October 1982 opponents of the extension occupied the field destined to be taken over for this purpose. A rota was set up in Oxford for people willing to go and spend the night at the occupation site, and Norman and I took turns at spending one night a week there.

At the beginning of 1983 my daughters were aged five and three. I still believed we could stop the arrival of the Cruise missiles that were due at the end of the year. It was to be an exhausting year, with the results of one activity running into preparations for the next. I used to read bedtime stories with one eye on the clock, because I was due to go out to a meeting; I rarely had time to invite the children's friends to tea; much of Norman's annual holiday was taken in the form of days off to look after the children. On certain days I had arrangements with friends to meet the children from school or playgroup if I couldn't. All the time the pressures of local campaigning continued relentlessly. It was a balancing act between assuring the short-term welfare and the long-term security of our children.

By the end of the year I had been arrested five times. The first was at a small spontaneous blockade at Greenham, where I continued to go on occasions when larger numbers of women were needed. The second and third times were at Upper Heyford, where work started on the extension site in February.

The extension of the base at Upper Heyford was a tangible example of nuclear proliferation on our doorstep. When I first received a message on the phone-tree that contractors were starting work there erecting the new fence, I immediately cancelled plans for a weekend visit to my parents-in-law, and my husband took the children by himself. Every day for over a week until the fence was completed, people went out from Oxford to join the people who were permanently camped on the site. Always in a non-violent way, we set out to obstruct the contractors, looking for opportunities to discuss with them and the police the reasons for our actions. This mainly took the form of lying down in front of fenceposts or tractors until we were dragged away across the muddy field by police. On some occasions the police were content to drag people away, and on others they chose to arrest them.

The first time I was arrested with several other people; we were all charged with 'breach of the peace', and taken straight from police cells in Banbury to the magistrates' court there. Tired, thirsty and dishevelled, we were refused an adjournment, and most people remained silent in court as a protest against this treatment. On being told that I was being bound over to keep the peace, I agreed to the bindover, adding that I would try to 'keep the peace' according to my understanding of the term.

When I was arrested a week later, again with other people and in the same circumstances, I didn't have to appear in court for three days and I had more time to prepare myself. As far as I remember, most of us in court that day were given a chance to explain our actions. It is rare in such court cases for people to try to obtain acquittals on 'technicalities'. Most people are only too happy to admit to what they did, stressing the moral imperatives behind their actions, or citing international laws which specifically condemn or outlaw weapons of 'mass genocide'.

I tried really hard to reach out to the magistrate as a person. I tried to share with him my sense of everything we stand to lose if nuclear weapons are ever used. It wasn't difficult to talk in this context of everything I love about the world; forced to spend so much time away from my children, I felt my motives as keen and ever-present as a raw nerve. Nowadays I think I would find it impossible to talk this way in court. I've heard people lay themselves bare in this way too often, only to be told that their motives are irrelevant, and to be charged with trivial offences, as if the magistrates have not even been listening. After a while, one's own deepest fears and convictions begin to sound like hollow clichés when repeated in such unsympathetic circumstances.

On this occasion, however, I was able to relate my fears for the future to what was happening at Upper Heyford, the proliferation of the nuclear arms race there. Only too aware that other people who share these fears can actually come to different conclusions, I tried to point out the inconsistencies behind the 'deterrence' theory and listed reasons why we cannot put our trust in it for ever.

When I sat down in the mud in front of a tractor, I knew that we could not hinder the construction work for more than a few days. But doing nothing is tantamount to giving one's consent; and the physical obstruction caused by our bodies was our way of withdrawing consent. I hope and believe that the moral impact of a group of people choosing this way to say 'no' to the destructive spiralling of the arms race must make itself felt in some degree not only on the bystander, but on anyone who later becomes involved: magistrates, police, neighbours. I felt I must say 'no' equally firmly when the magistrate sentenced me to be bound over to keep the peace. It was obvious from the court cases that had been continuing all week that the magistrates' definition of peace had nothing at all in common with ours; the wording of the charge, however, remained strongly ironic. I had known before coming to court what the inevitable consequences of a refusal to be bound over would be, and I had come prepared, with a packed suitcase.

That evening I was where I had expected to be, in the Reception wing of Holloway prison in London. On this occasion, the sentence of a week meant that I would spend six nights in prison. I had arrived in Holloway with another peace protester, Sarah, whom I had met at the occupation site at Upper Heyford. We spent the first night together in Reception, and then, although we were put in the same unit, we were in different cells, each of us sharing with one other woman. We were able to meet at meals, during the twice-daily walk round the exercise yard, and on the occasions when we were sent to work, packing toy tractors into boxes. This short stay seemed to bear very little relationship to any protest against nuclear weapons; rather it seemed a pause in the struggle, a time almost in limbo.

I could have continued my protest by refusing to work or refusing to co-operate in other ways, but I felt I did not want to set myself apart from the other prisoners, women much more qualified to talk about prison than I, who had the merest glimpse of what life must be like for them. There were long periods of being kept waiting outside the doors of doctors, or the assistant governor, who had to fill in yet another form;

doors were constantly locked or unlocked as I passed along a maze of corridors. Periods of confinement to my cell, already long, could be arbitrarily extended because of staff shortages, or because another prisoner in one's unit had infringed some petty rule. Many things had the effect of making me feel I was being treated as less than human. Even though time was mostly unfilled, meals had to be eaten in ten minutes or left unfinished; we were expected to address the warders as 'Miss'; on one occasion I had to remake my bed three times, until it was to the satisfaction of the warder. When I finally met with her approval, she immediately pulled it roughly apart so that another warder could go through the motions of searching it for drugs. Many of my letters were withheld from me and I only received them when I left the building. I knew the letters existed as I had already been shown the envelopes, and when I asked for them, I was given the excuse that as I had had so many letters, there was not enough time for the warders to read them all before giving them to me.

The idea of prison had not worried me at all. Other women, friends who had been there recently, had told me what to expect. What I found was an environment redolent of many of our Victorian hospitals. I was warm, I could have hot baths, and I suffered no physical deprivation. What disturbed me and made a lasting impression was the glimpse I had into the lives of the other women there. Surely they were less 'criminal' than the people who accrue riches by designing and promoting nuclear weapons; many of them were jailed on remand for months, merely awaiting trial. Others had committed very minor offences. Many suffered an apalling lack of self-esteem; and this was what the regime at Holloway seemed designed to perpetuate.

I talked to several women who were separated from their children. In a week I had occasion to feel homesick. The night after a visit from my husband and children, I cried myself to sleep. What could it be like for the other prisoners?

One thing turned that week in Holloway into a positive experience personally. It reinforced my protest against nuclear weapons and of the way in which all of us in that movement are linked in everything we do. My cell and Sarah's cell were full of flowers, some sent by friends, and others by people we had never met. In cards and letters, people from all over the country shared with us their fears and aspirations, but mainly their hope. Unlike so many women in Holloway, we were not isolated. I was grateful and sometimes amazed at the generosity of the other women prisoners, not only in the way that they guided us through the system, but in the way that they were able to admire our flowers without resentment.

On 20 March, four days after my release from Holloway, I was among 150 people attending a ceremony outside the extension site at Upper Heyford. We placed white crosses along the newly-completed perimeter fence. The sight of the fence was saddening, but we did not let our temporary defeat blind us to all the work that needed to be done.

Already we were planning and training, not only for the blockade which would take place the day before the big CND Easter demonstration, but also for the four-day national blockade of the Upper Heyford base which was planned for the beginning of June. On 31 March I was part of an Oxford affinity group blockading a road leading to the entrance of the nuclear weapons factory at Burghfield; similar blockades were taking place at other gates and at Greenham. This time, the response of the authorities to our strength was to let the day pass with a minimum of arrests.

In April I appeared in court at Newbury, charged with obstruction of the highway as the result of a blockade in which I had taken part in January. The courtroom was packed with women on similar charges, and their supporters. Again, those on trial were given a chance to speak, and deeply moving accounts of people's love for the world and their fears for its future stood harmoniously with well-reasoned pleas that minor infringements of local laws were justified when international laws were being flouted. My charge sheet read 'Obstruction of the Highway without due reason or excuse' and it was on this latter phrase that I based my defence. If a lorry were about to run over my child, I would be justified in placing myself between the lorry and my child. Again I tried to convey my conviction that nuclear weapons carried an equally real threat to all the world's children, and again the magistrate ostensibly refused to see further than local traffic laws. This time I was only fined ten pounds, and there was so much to be done and time was so precious that I eventually decided to pay the fine.

Between 31 May and 4 June, 730 people were arrested at the Upper Heyford Airbase. After months of preparation, people came from all over the country to blockade all five gates in the seven-mile long fence, different days and different gates being allocated to people from different areas. Norman had the week off from work and took the children on holiday so that I could live near Upper Heyford and help with the vast amount of support work which needed to be done, ensuring that legal backup was provided where needed, keeping track of people who had been arrested, giving out information, etc.

On the first day of the blockade, groups from Oxford were among others to be allocated to the main gate. Protesters were soon removed from this gate and police cordons stopped us from returning. Several attempts were made throughout the day to blockade the road at a point as near to the gate as we could get, and I was among the several people arrested as the result of these attempts. We were taken to a makeshift police station in a nearby marquee, and then in a police van to Banbury police station, until there were about seventy of us being held in a police gymnasium. I was released about 8.30pm, having been charged to appear in court later in the month. At this court appearance I pleaded not guilty and my trial, like the other not-guilty trials, was adjourned until August.

At the end of the four-day blockade, many of the people I had worked with were exhausted, but I felt the blockade had been a great success. In arresting so many people, in the first mass arrests since the 1950s, the authorities had been forced to acknowledge the strength of the opposition. The American nuclear base at Upper Heyford had been headline news. For the base to function at all normally that week, hundreds of ordinary people had had to be arrested. Even after seeing the people coming before them being dragged away and arrested, others had sat down to take their place. Our strength was obvious to ourselves and others, and it had increased.

The optimism we felt then did not last. I can't remember at what point during the year I began to admit to myself that we would not stop Cruise missiles. The general election in June, bringing back a Conservative government with a stronger majority, certainly was a factor.

In August our house was frequently full of people who had come to Oxford from all over the country to await trial in Banbury. The day before I appeared in court, the stipendiary magistrate, brought in specially from London, had stated that nuclear weapons were not, in his opinion, illegal. Several people had presented well-prepared defences to demonstrate the illegality of these weapons under International Law. Again, I personally tried to convey the reality of the threat of these weapons as I perceived it. I felt that the aspects of International Law had been more than adequately covered and I wished that the magistrate could make the imaginative leap from theories to facts. The nature of nuclear war is so terrible that many people retreat from thinking about it; how then can we ever expect a fair trial, when judges and magistrates react in this way too? Trying to explain what the nuclear threat meant to me, I wept. I talked of the images of Hiroshima and Nagasaki which haunted me, images I have related to my children. I was found guilty of obstructing the highway, and fined ten pounds with thirty pounds costs. I knew then that I had no intention of paying.

When, in November, I was sent to prison for refusing to pay the fine, the week's detention to which I had been sentenced was reduced by remission to two nights, one spent in Witney police station, and the next in Cookham Wood prison. Coming as it did at a time when so much was happening, this made very little impact on my life, and I can recall very few details of those two days. One encouraging aspect of going to prison, however, is the effect it has on other people. Several acquaintances, local shopkeepers for example, suddenly started to discuss nuclear weapons with me; that a few days in prison can provoke discussion of the issue, when the profound implications of the issue itself have previously failed to do so, amazes me. Similarly, people even closer to me, relatives whom I had asked to help look after the children while I was away, seemed to be listening to what we were saying for the first time.

That was in November. In October I had risked a heavier sentence. With the imminent arrival of Cruise more than likely, it had been decided to cut down as much of the perimeter fence as possible at USAF Greenham Common. We saw this as a creative rather than a destructive act, symbolic of releasing the land to its former peaceful usage. In the event, about a quarter of the nine-mile fence was removed. The group of us who went from Oxford had not taken the decision lightly. We had to face, for the first time for many of us, the possibility, even if not the likelihood, of a long prison sentence. Those of us with small children calculated the percentage of their short lifetimes that we might have to spend away from them. At that time, however, our awareness of the perils facing our children was heightened, and as we decided to cut that fence, we clung to each other for comfort. Of the many hundred women active that day, only a small number were arrested. Perhaps the authorities wished to avoid

45

the impact of so many people in court on charges of a nature which left no doubt as to the seriousness of their motives. Of the twelve of us who went from Oxford, only one woman was arrested. She spent a month in prison for refusing to pay the resultant fine.

By 9 November 1983 we knew that Cruise missiles had arrived. During the next few weeks, many of us were very busy. There were demonstration vigils, visits to Greenham, less confident attempts at cutting the fence. There were meetings to discuss the tracking of the Cruise missiles every time they left the base, a scheme which was eventually to become the current highly successful Cruisewatch organisation.

I had started waking at night, contemplating the possibility of nuclear war with sheer fright. Nothing, apart from resisting the nuclear threat, seemed worth doing. We had often talked of having a third child; now it seemed wrong to have brought two into the world. Almost harder than my initial coming to terms with the nuclear threat was coming to terms with the fact that the struggle would be a long one. We would not win in the short term. Gradually I became able to see things in perspective. The arrival of Cruise missiles had been a false deadline. Equally horrific weapons had existed long before Cruise and more horrendous ones might follow before the arms race was halted. We might not win, but we had to try. If we were to continue the struggle, we had to do so in a way that we could sustain through a lifetime.

In January 1984 I was arrested at a blockade of the command centre for Cruise missiles at High Wycombe. At the trial in February, the magistrate ruled that he would not accept or even listen to any defence based on moral or political arguments. This court bore no relationship at all to justice, and I refused to recognise the court by standing when I was told to do so. But we brought symbols of life and hope into the courtroom. A birthday cake for a friend who was one of the defendants portrayed a dove of peace above the computer at High Wycombe. Another defendant gave the magistrate a plant and asked him to watch it grow and contemplate the life in it; he agreed.

That day in court I already knew that I was pregnant and I cherished images of hope. 'A child for peace', a friend had said to me. Gradually I tailored my activities in the peace movement to the needs of my pregnancy. I did a 'night-watch' at Greenham, but I slept for most of the night. Soon we had to come off the telephone trees that were activated whenever Cruise left Greenham. Now that I was home more often, Norman had more time to help in the local campaign.

In June I took part in a blockade of Grosvenor Square, London to coincide with Ronald Reagan's visit to London, but there were no arrests. In July I was sentenced again to a week in prison for non-payment of a fine. Again this meant two nights, one in a white-tiled cell which reminded me of a public lavatory in a Victorian police station in Oxford, and one in Holloway. This time, although my stay in Holloway was short, my eyes were more fully open to the conditions of prison life.

I was examined callously, even sadistically, by a prison doctor, and that night, sharing a cell with three other pregnant women, I heard more about the miseries and cruelty of prison life, especially as they affect pregnant women. But I am sure that nobody in prison for a short time sees more than a fraction of that misery.

In October 1984 Eluned Mary was born. By the time she was one year old I was gradually becoming active in the peace movement again. Our other children were born before I had faced up to the threat of nuclear weapons. I gained the confidence to have Eluned because I knew that so many strong and lovely people were continuing the struggle. When it is their turn to stand back for a while, I hope that others will take their place.

CHAPTER FOUR

The West German Movement

WOLFGANG STERNSTEIN

Wolfgang Sternstein, a doctor of political science, was born in Germany in 1940, at the height of power of the Third Reich. His early life had a profound effect on his views on the subject of war and the establishment of national objectives by force or threat of force. To quote him: 'As a German I feel a responsibility for the immeasurable suffering that my nation has caused others in two World Wars. We cannot dissociate ourselves from this past history. We cannot accept the national inheritance of Goethe, Schiller, Kant, and Beethoven and, at the same time refuse the inheritance of Hitler, Göebbels, Göring and Himmler. However, we seem to have learned only one thing from two catastrophic World Wars: next time we have to be on the winning side - even if, next time, there will be no winning side.'

In the account that follows, Wolfgang describes his own involvement in the anti-nuclear movement in West Germany. Before that account we include a brief outline of the development of that movement, as described by Wolfgang himself.

Introduction

In the years 1980-83 the German peace movement experienced a resurgence. The aim was to prevent the deployment of new intermediate-range nuclear weapons, due to take place in the Autumn of 1983, by collecting signatures — the so-called Krefelder Appeal. During this period, in October 1982 and again in June 1983, mass demonstrations took place in Bonn involving 300,000 to 400,000 participants. Other actions included 'sit-ins' in front of nuclear weapons silos and a three-day blockade of the nuclear weapons rocket base at Mutlangen. This took place from 1 to 3 September 1983 and involved such well-known writers as Heinrich Böll and Günter Grass, as well as scientists, doctors, and priests. In addition, a fifty-mile long human chain was formed on 23 October 1983 from EUCOM, the Command Centre of the American military forces in Europe, near Stuttgart, to the Pershing II base at Neu-Ulm. Many other smaller demonstrations were also held. Despite this enormous demonstration of public concern, we did not manage to stop the deployment. The peace movement was exhausted and discouraged. Only a few refused to let themselves be demoralised. They started, in the summer of 1984, a campaign of civil disobedience which was to be continued until the weapons were removed. The activists — there are 400 at the present time — pledged themselves to take part, at least once a year, in a sit-in on the main road to the base at Mutlangen. Others have declared themselves willing publicly to encourage others to take part in these sit-ins, although to offer this encouragement is itself an illegal act.

Since 1982 at least 3,000 people have appeared in court for non-violent opposition to the deployment of Pershing II missiles. Most judges have regarded their actions as criminal and have fined them. Some thirty activists have refused to pay their fines and have had to serve up to three months in prison as a consequence. A few judges, however, have not sentenced such protesters, because their acts of protest were non-violent. This inconsistency of treatment has led to a disagreement within the judiciary itself, and a ruling on a crucial paragraph of the penal code has been sought from the high court.

The campaign of civil disobedience for disarmament organises blockades (sit-ins), especially on the main road to the Pershing II nuclear missile base at Mutlangen. These occur frequently, often after Mass. Priests and laity, doctors, writers, housewives, unemployed and professors all sit in the road to Mutlangen. From 8 to 10 May 1986 about 250 people aged over 60 blocked the main road to the base for three days. Only a few were arrested, most were carried away by the police. In June 1986, for the first time in German history, a group of judges took part in the blockade. Further blockades are planned.

Other forms of civil disobedience involve refusal to pay taxes. Withholding income tax is possible only for self-employed individuals because employees are taxed before receiving their wages. However, to show symbolic support for the civil disobedience campaign, some employees withhold 5.72DM (a penny per missile) from their motor tax. The government waits until the sum withheld accumulates to 20DM and then sends bailiffs to confiscate goods to that value. A more overt form of civil disobedience is practised by those who enter military bases to plant trees, flowers, or vegetables, or to erect crosses.

All of these actions of civil disobedience make an appeal. They encourage members of the peace movement to take part and, through mass disobedience, to oppose the wrongful acts of the government. They also keep the issue of the deployment of nuclear weapons in the public eye and cause members of government to question their own consciences on these matters. The final aim of the civil disobedience campaign is to get the majority of the electorate on the side of the peace activists. The appeal to the public mind is through political argument and to the public conscience through the willingness of those who practice civil disobedience to accept punishment for their beliefs.

A Personal History of Resistance

'I have arrived.' The warder locks the door behind me. I am in a cell, 9 feet by 12 feet, with bars on the window, two metal beds set 2 feet apart, a wash basin, a small table, two small lockers, a toilet, a radiator, and a metal door with a peephole. My cell mate, an animal liberator serving nine months for driving a vehicle without a licence, sits apathetically on his bed. He is not interested in communicating with me. This is my first (but certainly not my last) stay in prison. Despite a feeling that I had reached my immediate destination, this first stay in prison represented only a stage on a journey which, I hope, still has a long way to go.

The first stop on my way was my conscientious objection to military service, back in 1957, when I was eighteen years old. From the experience of violence in my youth I came to the conclusion that under no circumstances did I want to take part in the destructive business of war. But simply to be a conscientious objector was not enough. If not pressure, threat, punishment or violence as a means of resolving conflict, what then? In my search for an alternative I found non-violent action. I read the books of Gandhi, King, Camara, Luthuli, and the brothers Berrigan. Even so it was a long time, and after many detours and wrong turns, before I was eventually led away from a purely theoretical preoccupation with non-violent action to the practice of it.

I had intended to become a scientist. I wanted to do research, to study and to write books. But there was another inner voice which said: 'In a world that needs action, not talk, there are more important things to do. The most important thing about non-violent action is that one practises it.' For many years I had to live with this inner conflict. I studied and graduated with a degree in political science. I married and started my career. We have two sons, now 20 and 13 years old. At this time everything seemed to be developing in a conventional way. However in February 1975 I went on a research project, to Wyhl in South West Germany. Here the local people had successfully opposed, by non-violent means, the building of a nuclear power station. This experience changed my life. It marked the beginning of my 'criminal' career as a supporter of the Peace and Ecology movement.

My first imprisonment was as a result of a 'sit-in' at the EUCOM Command Centre of the American military forces in Europe, North Africa and the Middle East. EUCOM, which is near Stuttgart, was symbolically occupied by 380 peace activists on December 12 1982. For this action I was fined 400DM — which I refused to pay. As a result of this refusal I was imprisoned for four days. Since then I have taken part in over a dozen non-violent actions, sit-ins, go-ins and even a 'Plowshares' action.

To date fifteen 'Plowshares' actions have taken place, all in the USA except the seventh, which occurred in West Germany and was the one in which I took part. On 4 December 1983, at the end of a 500 mile march from the North Sea down to South West Germany, a group of four people entered an army area in Schwäbisch Gmünd. Here we used hammers and boltcutters to damage a Pershing II missile carrier. In the group were: Karin Vix, aged 20, Herwig Jantschik, 23, Carl Kabat, 51, O.M.I., a Catholic priest from the USA, and myself, aged 44.

The court case was heard in February 1985 and attracted quite a lot of attention. The presiding judge, in his summing up, said that he too (and he spoke on behalf of the court as well) considered that the missiles were lethal. The dialogue had to be continued, with the aim of banning them from German soil, but it was unacceptable that individuals should take the law into their own hands.

Herwig and I were fined 1800DM, and Karin Vix 300DM. Carl Kabat was not prosecuted. He returned to the USA, took part in the eleventh Plowshares action with Helen Woodson, his brother and fellow priest Paul, and Larry Cloud Morgan, and received an 18-year prison sentence as a result. My two German compatriots in the action at Schwäbisch Gmünd refused to pay their fines and served, respectively, 90 and 60 days in prison.

Now I work in Stuttgart as a freelance researcher into the subject of peace and conflict. I earn a little by lecturing and journalism. I also receive financial support from a few friends who believe in my work but, without the patient support of my wife and children, I could not continue in this way. I owe special thanks to my family and friends.

My philosophy can be explained in a few sentences. I believe that information, protest, demonstration and legal action are necessary, but at the same time I am convinced that in view of the danger that nuclear weapons hold for the human race, these may not be enough. Maybe it is too late to stop the destruction posed by these weapons. But if there is hope, it is through mass refusal and disobedience, by the people, towards any government which may contemplate the greatest possible crime − the murder of mankind. I know that the way to a world without weapons is very long and that we may take decades or even centuries to achieve it. Even so it is a goal worth living for, and, if necessary, dying for.

CHAPTER FIVE

Testament With Reason

MOLLY RUSH

Molly Rush is a Catholic mother and grandmother from Pennsylvania. She is the director of the Thomas Merton Centre, an independent ministry for justice and peace that was founded in 1972 and grew out of opposition to the Vietnam war.

In November 1985, in an interview with William O'Brien published in the American journal The Other Side *(reprinted here with permission), Molly Rush traced the influences that led her to engage in civil disobedience against the nuclear state.*

In the early morning hours of September 9, 1980, eight Christian activists entered General Electric's weapons-assembly plant in King of Prussia, Pennsylvania. In a matter of minutes, they hammered the casings of two Mark 12-A warheads — first-strike weapons — and poured a bottle of their own blood on the weapons and on nearby classified blueprints. They then sat down and began praying and singing until security officials and police came to arrest them.

One of those eight activists was Molly Rush, a Pittsburgh mother and grandmother. Her participation in this early 'Plowshares' action — based on Isaiah's prophetic call to beat swords into ploughshares — was a powerful episode in Molly's fervent vocation of peacemaking. It has since inspired a number of Plowshares actions and a deeper concern among many Christians throughout the country about the seriousness of the arms race.

Most people, especially those of us who haven't dismantled many nuclear missiles, agree that Molly Rush is an extraordinary person. But the power of her witness is that she is also a quite *ordinary* person — a mother of six children, a homemaker, and the wife of a Pittsburgh industrial worker. Her Plowshares action, for which she spent over eleven weeks in jail, was not the extremism of a flaming ideologue. It was an act of love for her family based on a simple but powerful conviction that the arms race threatens all families, as well as the whole of God's creation.

Today Molly faces mandatory sentences for her many acts of civil disobedience. Yet as long as she is free, she continues to be involved in countless peacemaking actions with Pittsburgh's River City Non-violence Campaign, organised by the Thomas Merton Centre. She also travels around the country giving talks and workshops, mobilising countless Christians to deeper awareness of gospel activism in a nuclear age.

Molly is a disarmingly charming person with a welcoming presence. Over a simple lunch in the kitchen of the Merton Centre, we talked about her pilgrimage to peace and her thoughts on Christian life in the nuclear age.

Q: What's a nice Catholic mother and grandmother like you doing dismantling nuclear missiles and serving prison sentences?

A: Actually, it started with my involvement in the civil-rights movement in 1963. I had four young kids at that time and had never been involved in any kind of politics at all. I belonged to a Christian mothers' group in our local parish when a black French-American priest came and talked about racism and his experience of it. Shortly after that, the Catholic Inter-racial Council group leafletted in our parish council. I tentatively sent in my five-dollar dues to see where it would go.

Q: Was that considered a renegade thing to do at that time?

A: Oh, yes! It caused quite a few waves in my family — not in my immediate family, though. My husband supported it, but my brothers and sisters thought involvement in the civil-rights movement was a terrible controversy. My mother supported the idea, and I think that helped.

Q: And shortly after that you became concerned about the Vietnam war?

A: That concern grew out of my work with the Catholic Inter-racial Council. My brother was in Vietnam, and the oldest of my four sons was approaching draft age — he was one of the last ones to get a high number on the draft lottery before they shut down the draft. So I really began looking at the war-and-peace issue. I had a direct feeling of responsibility for my son. I also wrote to my brother over in Vietnam and told him I was marching against the war, and he wrote back and encouraged me to continue.

Q: Did those kinds of concerns alienate you from the Catholic church at the time? Did you ever think of leaving the church?

A: Well, I went through a period of real anger toward the church, which isn't completely resolved. I still get angry when the church doesn't live up to its own teachings, particularly on the racial issue. I went through a period of self-righteousness on that one. And there was a lot of reason to be!

But also, in the middle of that period, Vatican II happened, and I was learning more and more about the responsibility of the Christian and the church as the people of God. I had gone to Catholic grade schools, and I was a very obedient daughter of the church — mother of six children and all that. So I think it was a real step for me to go from simple obedience to deeper understanding of responsibility in terms of obedience to God's law.

Q: Did you find support and community in your political activism?

A: The Catholic Inter-racial Council was essential to me because I did find other people there who understood and echoed my concerns. I was coming in contact with people with a lot of ideas and traditions, some involved in the struggles against racism, and also part of the liturgical movement.

As a young girl, I'd heard about Dorothy Day,[1] and I started to read more deeply into her writings. In fact, one of the first things I did when I took over as director of the Thomas Merton Centre was to present Dorothy Day with the Thomas Merton Award. That was a frightening experience for me! I was overwhelmed with the tremendous task of having to be up on the stage with hundreds of people and give someone like Dorothy Day an award!

Q: What led you to the Plowshares action?

A: I would have to say that it's been my work at the Merton Centre, which was a form of education. I learned a great deal about the arms race by going to seminars, having information coming across my desk every day, meeting people who were involved in struggling against the arms race, being put in touch with the work that Jonah House was doing.[2]

But going to jail and doing some of the things that other people were doing — that just seemed beyond my ken. At the same time, I believed that what they were doing was very necessary. I had friends who had gone to jail during the Vietnam-war era. I hadn't myself — I had children.

Then in 1979 I went to a retreat in Cleveland. Dan Berrigan was there,[3] plus Bill Kellerman, John Schuchardt, and quite a few other people involved in various kinds of resistance. We spent the weekend reflecting on the Epistle of James, and it turned out to be a very powerful time. It was the last step I needed to get the nerve to say, 'Well, I'm going to do something.'

Q: Something?

A: Well, at that point, the 'something' was to go to Sojourners.[4] I had to go to Washington for a meeting of Catholic peace-and-justice groups. While there I went with Sojourners to the hotel where they were protesting the arms bazaar. At the last minute I decided to join that protest. I got arrested and spent the night alone in the DC jail. It was really quite a powerful experience.

I kept in touch with people and brought Phil Berrigan to Pittsburgh for a retreat in early 1980, when plans were shared for a very serious witness, a kind of direct action at a nuclear weapons plant.

Q: How did you react to that idea?

A: I thought, 'Yes, that's right, that's logical, that's something that needs to happen.' From there began, I guess, five or six months of real wrestling with my conscience, of talking and struggling with the question, 'What should I do?'

From the beginning, I thought it important that women take part in any such action, so it would not be looked at as a counter-military action. A woman who was the mother of children might have some impact on how our action would be seen and understood. And I always felt that it couldn't be an act of desperation; it had to be something of hope. I was seeking hope for my children.

I was amazed at how much people didn't want to hear the facts about nuclear weapons. Friends of mine would put up barriers, shut out information. I was working as an organiser, trying to get through to them. I soon realised that the problem went a whole lot deeper than trying to educate people or simply going into political action. I think it really became a question of faith: how do we address the issue in faith in a way that allows people to hear and respond?

Q: How are nuclear weapons a question of faith?

A: The nuclear arms race is centrally a question of faith. It's a question of where one's trust goes: is it in this nation-state, with nuclear weapons, or is it in the God of power and might, the Creator, the one in whom we are to place our trust? Does it come out of a sense of fear of the enemy, or does it come out of the love that's demanded of us? Nowhere does the question get raised more clearly than with the issue of nuclear weapons, because they threaten all of creation, they threaten all of the future. They become, I think, a rejection of God.

Out on the picket line we've had more than one conversation with fundamentalists who insist that the weapons are God's will. I think that's just one way people have of not dealing with the reality. I think it's a subterfuge, a way of avoiding reality. That's what Jesus called us to be: a people who deal with reality. And that's why he called us not only to be peacemakers but to feed the hungry, the thirsty, to visit the imprisoned – he was calling us into reality. So we can't put up artificial barriers between ourselves and reality, even a reality as horrifying and as frightening as nuclear weapons.

It seemed to me at the time that one way of breaking through those barriers of fear would be actually walking into a nuclear-weapons components producer, actually seeing those weapons and doing something about them in a way that's clear and unmistakable. That felt important, because people don't believe that disarmament is possible.

Q: I guess one can play with the word 'reality' and come back and say, 'But in reality, what good do such actions do?'

A: I can only talk about the real effect they have for me. One thing I hadn't realised until I was actually hammering on those things was the mystique I had personally put on those weapons. I had really assumed they would be impervious and that I could hammer as much as I wanted and nothing would happen. I had this wild idea that, since they could travel beyond the atmosphere and come back and withstand the temperature, how in the world could my hammer do any harm?

It was important to me to see the dents right there on the warhead. It gave me a much clearer sense of the reality of the weapons. We try to put them out of existence by pretending they're not there. We assume that the security around them is so incredible that it's impossible to break through. It's all part of our mystique about nuclear weapons, that they are somehow beyond human comprehension and human contact.

Q: In many ways it sounds like a question of idolatry.

A: Yes, I think it's crucial to break through that idolatry and come to a real sense of human contact. For a housewife without many hammering skills — at best hanging up a curtain rod — it really means something to take a hammer to one of those things. And my experience was that that action really meant something to many, many people who heard about it — I'm talking about hundreds of people who wrote to me, people I've talked to, people in this community I've been in touch with, and also around the country. My action really served as a catalyst.

Q: Some people feel that the Plowshares actions have a quality of violence in them.

A: That's a valid concern, and I think it needs to be addressed seriously. I think the first question concerns the definition of violence. Would governments disarming nuclear warheads be acting violently if they took them apart? If not, then it seems almost absurd that individuals doing the same thing are seen as violent.

Part of it is the framework of legality we've put around nuclear weapons. They are legal instruments, just as the gas ovens in Nazi Gemany were legal instruments. The Nazis didn't break the law by building them. Ordinary people felt they could participate in building them without breaking the law.

But that 'construct' of legality which underlies the arms race defies international law. The true basis of law is the protection of the community, and these weapons violate that law at every step of the way. But we disregard the true law and accept the legality of weapons. So hammering on them by an individual and not a government is seen as violent.

I think the other question about violence is, are you threatening or harming another human being or creation in the process? And

58

I think it's fair to say that that is not what happens when you hammer on a warhead — any more than hammering on a curtain rod endangers the creation of wood.

Q: You once said that because of your involvement with the Plowshares actions you have a greater sense of the preciousness of life and of joy. But when we involve ourselves in the reality of our world, we encounter so much injustice, so much violence, and so much despair. How do you discover that preciousness of life, that joy, in a violent world?

A: Well, I think that's a central question for peacemakers, because we can be violent to ourselves and to our families. It's always necessary to remain whole and human and to allow ourselves the time and energy to appreciate things like the sun above us, the grass and flowers at our feet. Sometimes these things get taken away from us — as they were from me in jail. Not being able to go outside was really the hardest thing for me — other than separation from family. It was so hard not to get outside in the sun and the rain and everything — just to be shut up. But you begin to appreciate them. I remember even appreciating the strip of sunlight that used to go across my cell wall at a certain time of day. It would change colours with the sunset. I think most of us spend too much time acquiring things, spending time with busyness, that we lose that appreciation.

That's why Thomas Merton is important to my life. His perspective of the need for prayer and contemplation is central. He could accept being human. And he was never afraid to enjoy a drink and a good laugh. I think that's essential.

Q: Is spirituality an ongoing part of your activism?

A: I'd say it's more central than ever. I would describe my participation in the Plowshares action as an act of personal conversion, making real those words in the gospel. Letters from men who were themselves in jail take on a whole new dimension. There's a contemplative side of jail, the ability to sit down and listen to others in jail, to hear their experiences and their situations as being very important. That's something people don't appreciate about the jail experience.

Some people have spent years and years in jail — Helen Woodson of the Silo Pruning Hooks, who just got eighteen years, Nelson Mandela in South Africa, people all over the world whose names we don't know. Somehow, a community happens with those people. It's very moving.

Q: What do you think is the place of civil disobedience in the Christian life, both for individuals and for the church as a whole?

A: When we're talking about a world that's threatened by war — not only nuclear war but conventional war — and people are dying every day because of the bombs and the troops we're funding, I think that becomes a more and more serious question. When you're faced with refugees from wars and the necessity of behaving as Christians, when you're faced with the question of taxes and the government's priorities — I don't think anyone can let themselves off totally.

That's not to say that everyone ends up in the same place. But I've heard too many people say, 'You are this special kind of person; you can do this, and I can't.' Too many people attempt to separate out the extraordinary folks from the ordinary ones. I don't know anyone who's gone to jail for civil disobedience who doesn't have his or her share of faults, fears, tremblings, and all that.

In prayer and in deep confrontation with our own vocations and callings, *what* are we asked to do? The answers can come out differently for different folks. What's happening recently with the Pledge of Resistance[5] is an incredible sign that all kinds of ordinary folks can come up with a willingness to take some kind of risk.

I don't think we should be the judges of what we're capable of doing. God provides a tremendous amount of grace when we're willing to let go and not be the judge. And when we're willing to hear the calling of our conscience.

Q: So much of the conservative Christian presence in this country places a strong emphasis on family. They might criticize civil-disobedience activists by saying, 'You have a family to support.' Since you yourself are a mother and grandmother, how would you respond to those Christians?

A: I'm a family person. I have seven brothers and sisters. I have six children and two grandchildren — three, come December. I can't think of anything I've done in my life that's more important to my family than the Plowshares action.

I think the kind of vision of family we need is not the narrow vision that opts us out of our larger responsibilities, but the sense that we're all part of the human family. If we're Christians, we can't ignore the families that are dying, the children that are dying. There are answers in community to some of these questions. And I think that's the challenge of Christian community and Christian families within communities: not to have such a narrow idea of our responsibility as parents that we lose our sense of responsibility for the world.

Q: The recent vote (in Congress) for aid to the Contras in Nicaragua dramatized how so often our efforts seem inadequate. For a lot of Christians, one of the most important questions is that of hope. What do you think are some tangible sources of hope?

A: I think the temptation is to look for positive signs that will help us to continue. That's important, but for me the most important thing is to separate out the whole question of optimism and pessimism from hope and despair. I think there are times when we're not going to see any reasons for optimism. But that's when we're called on to hope, that's the gospel call to hope — when we don't see hope. So I've come to see hope as a decision, as a choice. And it's a choice based on faith. When you're acting in hope, then hope becomes possible. If you're just standing there paralysed and not seeing hope, it's not going to come. Merton's been so good at teaching us about not looking for the end results of what we do, but to do right and know that fruit will come from these actions.

Q: Where do you see yourself years from now? Will you be doing the same kind of peace work?

A: Well, if I am, that will mean that we haven't all died from a nuclear war, which will be a good thing!

I don't know. I get tired sometimes, and I'd like to take a rest. But I know that probably wouldn't be satisfying for very long. I think we have to find joy in what we're doing. I know in recent months some good things have happened in Pittsburgh. I think we've had some interesting breakthroughs, especially in our negotiations with Westinghouse (over first-strike weapons production) and the non-violent training of the steel-workers (through the Tri-State Conference on Steel). I'm pleased to find myself getting excited after all these years.

I sense a deepening understanding of non-violence that I think has to capture our lives. I keep talking to college students about the real frontier of work that has to be done in the area of non-violence. It's exciting to see that they are beginning to understand. It's like the beginning of a whole revolution that has to happen. I hope I'll be part of that in some way.

Notes

1. *Dorothy Day*: Founder of the *Catholic Worker* in 1933. For nearly fifty years, until her death, she served the poor with a soup kitchen and hospitality house in New York City. There are Catholic Worker houses in many US cities. The *Catholic Worker* newspaper is pacifist, as was Dorothy Day.
2. *Jonah House*: a resistance community in Baltimore, Maryland, which has led the way in religious civil disobedience in opposition to nuclear weapons. Philip Berrigan, his wife Elizabeth McAlister, and other members of the community, have been jailed repeatedly for protests at the Pentagon.
3. *Daniel Berrigan*: Dan and his brother Philip were well known in the 1960s for opposition to the Vietnam War. They were jailed a number of times for resistance to the war, as in the 'Catonsville Nine' case, when they were sentenced to prison for burning draft board files. Dan is a priest, writer, and poet. His latest book is *Steadfastness of the Saints*, chronicling a recent visit to Central America.
4. *Sojourners* is a magazine arising from a 35-member community in Washington DC. It is 'a voice for change and a meeting place for people from diverse backgrounds who are turning their lives toward the biblical vision of justice and peace'.
5. *The Pledge of Resistance*: In June 1985, 2,000 people across the USA were jailed for protest against US funding for the 'Contra' guerrillas in Nicaragua.

CHAPTER SIX

An Empty Cartridge

PETER LUCAS ERIXON

Peter Lucas Erixon is a young Swede who, like many of his fellow countrymen, refused to do his military service and went to prison as a consequence. In correspondence he tells us that he does not come from a family with a pacifist tradition or strong religious convictions. Nevertheless, while in prison, he had a lot of support from friends and people near him and letters from parents, authors, and from other resisters. His objection to war is based on both political and religious grounds but he summarises his attitude by saying '...that my reason for resisting the draft was — and is — simply human. There are things you do and things you do not. War is totally anti-human and has nothing to do with real human life.'

It is hard to know for sure if there are today more or fewer young men in the world who refuse to do military service. Now and then statistics are published — but these can hardly measure a genuine will to resist; tables cannot reveal the depth of genuine anti-military feeling in many countries around the world.

I, like hundreds of others in Sweden, have rejected compulsory military service and the fraudulent alternative known as weapon-free duty. From my middle teens, my thoughts were frequently occupied by the approaching and inevitable conscription order. I knew that one day, the envelope would turn up in my mail. And that I would be forced to face a situation which for a young inexperienced person is truly no minor matter. Conscientious objectors to military service have to find the courage for an encounter with The Dragon. They declare their defiance against a whole State, a whole way of thinking, a whole military organisation, the whole system of national 'defence'. And this is no easy task. Still, there are several hundred men each year in Sweden who simply cannot accept the fact that automatically, without their consent, they are conscripted for military training. And although I have said that I am sceptical of statistics, I none the less feel satisfaction every time I see that the number of objectors has increased. And I say to myself: At last! True resistance is rooting itself here! Now we can begin to hope for something.

As I turned the age of sixteen, I had had very little experience of life. I felt an extraordinary horror of systems in general and of military systems in particular. And most of all, I had a horror of the Swedish conscription authorities, who would one day enter my name on their lists. One day my name would be chosen by that mindless computer.

With every year that passed, the time was inevitably approaching. At sixteen, my name was entered into the conscription computer. Seventeen, eighteen, nineteen — suddenly the order was in my hand. During those years I had managed — how, I don't know — to acquire some sort of moral courage. I was prepared to take on The Dragon, to throw myself into that gigantic machinery, refuse before witnesses to take up arms, defend my position before the courts, pay the fines, resist once more, be called up again, defend myself publicly, and be jeered at.

So then — in my nineteenth year — my story of public resistance began. It began with an unbelievable night. I was to report to one of Sweden's most northern small towns. Which meant I would have to leave my home and my girl friend the evening before. I was anxious and deep in thought, without any hope — but some strange reserve of strength kept me going, like a car with its engine disengaged. I said to Christina: 'Make sure that a candle shines for me tomorrow to spread some ray of hope over this miserable episode.'

The train was crowded with other recruits. I had reserved a seat, but all were occupied, and I didn't have the strength to find mine and ask someone else to leave it. So I alternated between standing and squatting for twelve hours, and tried to concentrate on preparing myself for the coming ordeal, while getting more and more exhausted. Still I remember vividly the scenery that June night as the train made its way through northern Sweden, with the crossing signals giving warning and the cars sweeping past out there. And when we stopped at a station — I don't remember which, I was in a daze in this unbelievably trying situation — I saw a steel-blue beam of light from a lamp somewhere: from somewhere on the platform a searchlight was pointed directly towards me where I perched. A steel-blue ray of light, and the June night's own special illumination, out there. Voices, drunken boys, new faces flowing constantly past me where I perched. I recognized one of the boys, a classmate from home — but I didn't greet him. I was in a world of my own and had finally reached the absolute conviction that I, just recently turned nineteen, would change the world and the traditional ideas that continued to rule it: the notion that a few have the right to be masters over others, and force them to undergo military training, totally unnatural, in order to learn the most rational and efficient methods of killing.

And so I reached my destination. Morning came. And it was time for me to find my way to one of the military camps in the town. I had been selected for training as a squad commander, and was eagerly awaited. So when I showed up, I was greeted with nothing but smiles.

'And what is your name?'

'Erixon.'

'Erixon ...'

He looked through his papers.

'Good! Come along then!'

He was pleased. The main part of the group had assembled, and I was one of the last. Now he was to give me my instructions. I felt a little sad about having to disappoint him, when he had welcomed me so warmly.

'Ah ...'

I tried to catch his attention.

'You see, I'm ...'

And I thought to myself: Now. Now I must say it — that tremendous moment which I had been waiting for and preparing myself for during four long years!

'You see, I don't intend to take part in this.'

Surprise. Commotion. Clear disappointment showing in his face. But rational action!

'Come along!'

He ran ahead with me at his heels up to his office; and then a long wait. And I thought: Now they are surely going to be angry with me. But no. I have seldom been so decently treated by any public institution as I was at this time. Of course there were one or two of those whom I was forced to meet that day who treated me, and spoke to me, as though I were an idiot. I remember especially a woman who acted in a rather peculiar and annoying manner.

'Oh, dear! Oh, dear! How can you have such ideas! What do you mean by this?'

And she whispered to a male colleague: 'And he says he is a writer!' She asked me what I had written, how I could have such ideas, whether I understood what the consequences of my action would be. I answered dutifully and succeeded quite well in remaining composed. I explained that I was rather new as a poet, that my first book had not yet come out. What did I think about my situation? I believed that this refusal was the sole contribution I could make in this world, which was rushing on through the universe at a speed of 9,000 knots, burdened with astronomical military budgets, military organizations so devilish and unnecessary that now only the stupid and the foolhardy can actually survive here. I mean simply that I cannot give any part of my time or energy to a military apparatus whose only goal is ultimately to eradicate other human beings, just as alive, afraid, decent, and hard-working as I.

But all of this mockery mattered so little now that at long last I had worked my way up to the starting line and was on my way in the first lap of my resistance to military service.

And even this period came to an end. I was sentenced at the trial five months later to a fine and probation — all in line with the present practice.

June came again. In 1982 it was time to report a second time, to the same regiment. In December the court of appeal sentenced me to a prison term of four months — exactly what I had expected all along.

And then followed a long winter of waiting day after day for word informing me where I was to report. The letter came in April 1983. I was to do my four months at an open State prison in central Sweden. Together with arsonists, rapists, drunken drivers, safe crackers, and a few other fellows. Altogether, there were a little more than one hundred inmates.

My four months began on 20 May 1983. Just a week before I was to report, I heard a welcome announcement on the radio. The Swedish government had decided, because of the shortage of prison accommodation, that all people with sentences under two years — whatever their offence — would have their terms reduced by a half. So my prison sentence became two months instead of four.

Well, well, it was like an adventure out of some boys' book. It was a warm summer, and the first half was not too bad. In the evenings I carried on with my own work. I wrote, corrected, and put papers in order. And I made plans for life after my release.

I lived these two months in a cell measuring two by three metres. A bed, a table fixed to the wall, an orange plastic chair, a washbowl, a radio receiver connected to the central system, a closet, and a bookshelf. During the day I worked at a boring job in the carpentry shop, spray-painting shelves, machine-finishing edges, and other similarly monotonous tasks. During breaks I played cards and pondered on my situation, or smoked with a Yugoslav who was there for assault (second time), another draft resister, a man in for drunken driving, and some others not so clear in my memory.

One day when we came back to the workshop after lunch, men in black uniforms and with German shepherd dogs were in the locker room. It was a special commando unit which was checking that we did not have drugs on us. I didn't have any. But I felt so strongly that those fellows looked like soldiers I had encountered in South America three years earlier (on a bus in Colombia, awakened abruptly in the middle of the night, dragged out and searched), that I said:

'This is like South America.'

The fellow who had just checked that I hadn't hidden a one-kilo hashish cake or a M-16 in my anus exploded in anger. He was in no mood for jokes — one could see that in his eyes. He shouted something at me. He was furious. But he did not bother me again — he just shoved me out of the way.

At breakfast almost every day a peculiar man came to my table. He would sit down beside me. Each day he had at least one stolen watch on his wrist. He had silver-grey hair, and grey eyes. He teased and provoked me.

'Ah!' he would say.

'You should have seen Nürnberg!' He said. And smiled and smiled.

67

'There! There we were many millions! And if you had been there — we executed the likes of you immediately! Those were the days!'

He spoke with a whispering voice and charmingly provocative eyes, and a smile that revealed that he was just a little unbalanced and needed someone to wrangle with. I knew I had nothing to fear from him. So instead we laughed together — I at him because he was comical, extraordinary, and quite simply absurd, as he sat there rambling away. And he laughed at me because I was an 'empty cartridge' — the Swedish prison slang for war resisters — and must have been quite a sight: very skinny, tired, and dressed in green, my hair cropped. But all in all I was relieved that the atmosphere in the prison was not violent for the most part: it was mainly quite fraternal and just.

And so the summer of 1983 passed by. My experience of resistance was at an end. On 20 July 1983 I was once again a free man.

Still today I live with the firm belief that my one-man witness did, and does, make a difference. Everyone's contribution has a value. And I am absolutely sure that refusal to do military service is the greatest threat than can be offered to military systems all over the world.

Your life is yours as soon as you yourself want it to be so.

CHAPTER SEVEN

Suffering is an Act of Life

ELIZABETH McALISTER

Elizabeth McAlister, a mother of three young children, is married to Phil Berrigan. Both are veterans of the anti-Vietnam war protest of the 1960s and early 1970s. Before her marriage she spent two years in a religious order, attempting to fulfil her desire to serve society in a more direct way than that of wife and mother. She emerged from this period with a deep love of Scripture and with strong pacifist convictions. For her, rationalizations about the containment of Communism could not justify widespread killing in war: Christ, and not the Presidency, was 'the way, the truth and the life'. These pacifist values led Liz to join others who held similar views and, by the end of the Vietnam war in 1972, she had been to prison repeatedly for her non-violent opposition to the conflict.

In Syracuse, New York, on Thanksgiving Day 1983, Liz and six others disarmed a B-52 bomber equipped to carry Air Launch Cruise missiles. For this action Liz received a three year prison sentence. In interviews since her imprisonment she has spoken, with feeling, of the need for her and her husband to explain to their children why she chose to carry out an act that was inevitably going to lead to a prolonged separation from them. Despite the distress this separation caused her, she is resolved to continue with her peace-seeking. She is aware of her limitations — she says, of an earlier anti-war protest at the Pentagon: 'Facing the power there was an awesome thing. The best within me despairs... I am still a child in regard to Scripture; I have doubts, a sense of impotence, so often.'

The following article is a short excerpt from the testimony that Liz gave at her trial for the Thanksgiving Day action.

In going to prison I face separation from my children. Why do I take this risk? Being a parent makes the need for protest more essential —

but more difficult. However, I believe firmly that the major issue of concern to parents today must be the prevention of nuclear war. For this reason I must accept the separation from my children though I find it difficult to do so. I have three choices: First, to go to a safe place .. that is no option. Second, pretend that the threat is not there: not to read, not to think. Or third, ask how I can best love them, give them some hope for the future? ... Do something to make that future a reality.

Do my children understand? With our two elder children Phil and I saw the television documentary 'The Day After'. We discussed it with them and we used it to explain that I would be involved, in the coming week, in an action to prevent nuclear war. We explained that the action would bring deprivation and probably involve my being in prison for some time. They expressed their willingness to accept the personal sacrifice of my absence as their contribution, and they agreed to help look after the home while I was away. It was a moment of extreme closeness for the four of us, a moment of accepting together whatever might happen, and we concluded our conversation with prayer and big, big hugs. Maybe it was a moment when, as a family, we tried to share some of the dignity of entering the real world — the other world where suffering is a fact of family life. It is to their credit that they said 'yes' to that. We all back down from moments like that ... but we don't back down completely. Something of the clarity of a moment like that stays with us, enlightening a dark time. While they fear prolonged separation, they are proud of their mother, and of themselves, for offering something, for sharing something of the suffering of people in less privileged circumstances.

In 1975 I saw, for the first time, the documentary film called 'Hiroshima and Nagasaki', a sixteen minute film with footage from the bombing and victims of that bombing. The film had, and continues to have, a terrific impact on me. I cannot watch it and not think about how I would behave if it were my child suffering as some of those children suffered. I made a commitment. If I am not prepared to see my children suffer as they did, then I must do something.

There now follows a brief extract from Liz McAlister's closing statement:

Why did we risk being maimed or killed or sent to prison? ... we looked at our very real fears — there is nothing especially courageous about any of us — and we tried to hear the Biblical mandate, 'Don't be afraid: only have faith'. We tried to learn from that command that a spirit of simple obedience removed from us the worry of success, of effectiveness. We understood in some simple but real way that our effort to be faithful could free the promise of God to be effected. In some way that we couldn't understand, it would enable the spirit of God and his peace to be released in our World in a new and real way to effect the miracle.

CHAPTER EIGHT

'What Did You Accomplish?'

PAUL KABAT

Paul Kabat is a 55 year-old American Catholic priest. He played an active part in the anti-Vietnam war protests during the 1960s and early 1970s and has, since that time, become involved in the 'Ploughshares and Pruning Hooks' movement of protest against nuclear weapons.

In November 1984, as one of the 'Silo Pruning Hooks' group, he attempted to disarm a nuclear missile silo in Missouri. His co-defendants at the subsequent trial — Helen Woodson, his brother and fellow-priest Carl, and an American-Indian, Larry Cloud Morgan — received prison sentences ranging between eight and eighteen years. Paul himself was given a ten-year sentence (later reduced to five years). He was released in March 1987.

This article, written in prison, attempts to answer the question 'what did you accomplish?' It is included to dispel any idea that Father Paul is naive in his assessment of the opposition that the peace movement faces.

Perhaps one of the most demoralising questions to be asked of an activist like me about our recent act of disarmament of a nuclear missile silo is, 'What did you accomplish?' It's like asking a young couple shortly after the birth of their first baby, 'What did you accomplish?'

The simplest answer to that question is that we hope we have made a significant contribution to the future of humanity. Obviously any accomplishment is still very much in the future, 'in via', on the way.

Perhaps the fact that the question is being asked by some is already part of our accomplishment, although we of the Silo Pruning

Hooks hope that our action is not just relegated to that question alone, to become a minor footnote in a future obscure history book — if there will be a future for such a history book to be written.

Although in my wildest fantasy I may have hoped that our effort of disarmament would have already turned the dynamics of world and national politics around, in my more rational moments I am aware that we may have had little impact on anybody or anything. Whatever impact we may have is lost in the abundance of distractions that people have in order to keep themselves alive or entertained — or whatever is important to them from day to day.

In spite of my fantasies, I do not expect my act or my resulting years in prison will have any cosmic effect on history, just as I am aware that the quiet deaths of many children in fourth-world situations around the world make no real difference to us Americans, and especially to the political and economic leaders of our nation. Millions of children phase out silently and are buried in obscurity, so we will not be much noted as time and events go by.

Being realistic, I know that most Americans are not aware of our action, and do not even want to know about it. If I were to run for a national office, I would have no recognition at all. Certainly I am no Ted Kennedy or Gary Hart, nor a Jesse Jackson or a Geraldine Ferrara. Nor am I a Pete Rose, or a Joe Montana, or a Chris Evert Lloyd, or a Madonna, or whoever is being featured on the cover of 'People' Magazine this week, this month, or this year.

Does this mean that unknown people like you and me should sit back and let the world go by without us as we eat, drink, and survive from day to day until some form of death brings us to our interment?

Success is not measured by passing notoriety or some kind of public recognition. My success is to live an authentic and humane life to the best of my ability. For me it was humane and authentic to try to disarm a nuclear missile at N-5 near Kansas City, Missouri, before it was discharged towards some distant target to kill millions of my fellow human beings.

I wish thousands of other Americans would join me in similar acts of disarmament to put a stop to the arms race and to discourage our political and economic leaders from destroying the human race. There seems to be no other way to bring the insane nuclear arms race to a halt, to turn the process of omnicide around. Every day our stockpile of nuclear arms grows by three or more weapons in this country. Every day we travel deeper and deeper into the state of insanity.

As far as I know, the four of us Silo Pruning Hooks are the first people ever to try to disarm a loaded nuclear facility directly. Even though we knew there was six feet of concrete between us and the missile, and that our efforts would be more symbolic than effective, we felt that somebody had to make a first move towards productive disarmament. We knew we would never get near the warhead, even if we could have been on the site for a week, much less the few minutes we were actually there. We still had to make some kind of effort to disarm that nuclear bomb.

So what did we accomplish, and what will we be accomplishing by our life in prison? Who knows?

At least we are a continuing testimony of our concern for humanity and for real disarmament. Because we are religious people, we hope we have had some redemptive value for eternal life, as well as intercessory power before the throne of God.

Because we are thinking and acting people, we hope we are having a thoughtful and productive effect on other thinking and active people.

Because we are human beings, we hope we are bringing more humanity into a world going mad with many forms of violence and oppression.

Maybe we will not accomplish anything of cosmic worth by our efforts and our imprisonment. Maybe little will be changed and little remembered of what we tried to do.

However, I know what I did and why I did it. I feel more human and more authentic and even more productive than I ever did before in my life. I hope I can be satisfied with those results. Whatever else may be produced is 'extra wurst' (extra sausage), as Father Chester Kozal, OMI, used to say. That good man and teacher of mine survived some years in the Dachau concentration camp. I hope I can survive five years in an American prison system and can do whatever God is calling me to do and to be.

With that I will leave the final accomplishment to God. 'Not my will but yours be done.'

CHAPTER NINE

A Question of Values

ARTHUR WINDSOR

Arthur Windsor is a retired librarian who lives in Gloucester. He and his wife Ursula, who are both Quakers, have for several years expressed their moral objections to war by withholding the proportion of their income tax that is levied for military purposes. Their efforts to divert forty-five per cent of their income tax to spending on social welfare resulted in a three-week prison sentence for Arthur in 1986 — the first such penalty for a 'peace tax' campaigner in Britain.

The extent to which our childhood experiences affect our later life has been made clearer to me on reflecting on my life of nearly seventy years. The attitudes of the last forty of these have, for me, been radically conditioned by the dawning of a new spiritual awareness that all is of a piece: Christian faith, practical life, and aspirations towards social justice, peace and non-violence. To throw light on this, I must go back.

At the age of eight, I crossed over to France for the first time, with my mother and aunt, in a Toc H party going to view the war-graves in the battlefields of Flanders. This was in 1925, six or seven years from the end of the first World War. Some damage was still visible in Arras, where we stayed, and in the surrounding country. The impression was of a catastrophe that had passed but had left deep marks. We visited my father's grave at Souchez, where the wooden cross, made by his comrades, still stood. Near Vimy Ridge we saw a large dugout with an unexploded shell embedded in its 'roof'. The thing that made the greatest impression on me (apart from the hotel atmosphere: a combination of soup and cigars) was the waiter's writing my age ('huit ans') in pencil on the tablecloth after dinner.

In our ordinary life as children at home, books, squeaky 78 r.p.m. records, and mementoes of 'heroes of the War' — such as my uncle's embroideries of flags and my father's of his regimental badge, done when he was wounded and in hospital — reminded us of the nearness of the Great War, as it was then called. I was an only child, posthumous, but lived near and played with a large family of cousins.

As November 11, Armistice Day, came round each year, my mother would bring out and look at my father's medals: the 1914 Star (which was his as one of 'Kitchener's Army'), the Service Medal, and the Victory Medal, none of which he knew about; he was killed in 1916. Some time in my early teens the Imperial War Graves Commission replaced the hand-made crosses by carved headstones; the cross I had seen in France was sent to my mother, who kept it in the 'gas cupboard' under the stairs in our railway cottage. Its cracked surface, black lettering, and the few remains of French mud at its base seemed to me to typify, in a baleful way, a range of pious, mournful, and admiring sentiments which I found difficult to share, never having known my father, other than as a presence in a photograph album, or as a shadowy personality behind the pencilled notes at the back of a Bible I inherited from him.

Later, in the sixth form at school, I took part in a debate aimed at such pious observances as Armistice Day, which I then openly forswore with some heat, though feeling at the time, a little uncomfortably, that I might be betraying something that was dear to my mother. This was as far as I ever went, publicly, in the direction of pacifism. I am speaking now of the mid-1930s, when Hitler had come to power and the Spanish Civil War was about to start, when the young became anti-fascist in spirit. I had been brought up as a devout Baptist, but my church seemed unaware of the real social and political issues, especially those of war and peace. I began to drift away very gradually from my earlier faith.

By the time I started library work in 1936, I began to take a left-wing position, which caused a severe dilemma for me by 1939, the beginning of the war, for I was due to be conscripted in 1940.

On the one hand I felt that war and arms were evil, on the other that Hitler and his regime were evil also. My church took a 'patriotic' attitude and was no help. So I was called up and served six years in the army, in an undistinguished way, first in the Pioneer Corps, and then in REME. During the second half of my service I was stationed in Sri Lanka—then known as Ceylon—where I experienced two bouts of malaria.

In hospital during one of these, I had what I think of as a mystical experience. I felt I was taken up to the top of a very high mountain, from which I had a God's-eye view of the world and of the war. I could see, stretching away to the horizon, two vast, grey armies locked in unprevailing conflict, neither able to overcome the other. Their anonymity seemed to emphasize the senselessness of the conflict; had either been the victor, its identity would have been immaterial; the victor, in either case, would have been equally unrelenting towards the other. I saw the madness of it and cried out to God to put an end to it, or rather to induce mankind to do so. This was a year or so before the atom bombs were dropped. After Hiroshima and Nagasaki (I was in hospital in India at the time) my conviction of the sin of war was enhanced. I had never had to take any active part in the war, and during the two years before my discharge, my increasingly pacifist convictions grew. At the same time my Christian faith also began to return; it had been in abeyance during my earlier army life.

In 1946, when I was discharged from the army, and returned to library work, I met Ursula Valentin, a German refugee of Jewish parentage but Christian religion, who was working at the same library as I, and within a year we had married. It was largely through her influence and strong faith that I fully regained my own faith. My first outing to London with Ursula was mainly to go to Tower Hill to hear Donald Soper speak. This I continued to do during the following year, when I was a student in London. His ministry was one of the main formative influences on me at the time: his rational yet eloquent and moving exposition of the Christian stance not only towards war and peace but also to social justice and political awareness was most important to me. I must be one of many who are, without his knowing it, greatly indebted to him. Another influence at that time was the series of meetings for ex-servicemen held by the Central Board for Conscientious Objectors. I was trying to find some way through the problem of being asked to do 'Z Reserve' service, as an ex-serviceman. I found it: I would become a C.O. now. I wrote to the War Office to say that I would not do the service and that from now on I was to be considered as a Conscientious Objector. I had no reply. Within five years Ursula and I (she a Methodist, I a Baptist) had together joined the Society of Friends (Quakers). From this time on we considered ourselves as pacifists and always acted together in the social and political sphere. As we brought up our family, we tried to adopt a life-style expressing our newly-realised convictions. Within another three years we had met Lewis and Sarah Benson, American Quakers, whose message and example have radically affected our life and, particularly, our view of the significance of our Quaker faith. We began to see that if Christ rules our lives as a community, so also he rules our individual and family lives. We tried to find the true life of the church, in fellowship with others who were doing the same. This took us to Gloucester in 1962 to share our lives with two other families, within the general pattern of the local Quaker Meeting.

Just before this, in 1955-56, we were sponsored by Quakers to go to live, with our young family, in the Soviet Union, possibly Moscow, as a gesture of reconciliation and something of a bridge between British Quakers and the 'East', in the thaw that was just beginning. But this was not to be, although we took Russian lessons and I attempted to get a library job in Russia. All this time, internationally, suspicion and distrust between East and West were building up: secret agreements affecting the development of the A-bomb, then the H-bomb, and the beginning of the arms-race, all had their subtle effect on our lives as ordinary people. The growth of CND seemed a break-through at the time, and we went with our family on the early Aldermarston marches. But who did not feel powerless and frustrated in the face of growing demonic forces over which we seemed unable to have any influence? The 1960s, with their student unrest, and the 1970s passed and the environmental movements grew, while the idea of non-violent direct action began to seem a positive way of backing up our protests.

We first became aware of the tax issue when for a few years Ursula and I were both working and paying far more income tax than before. I retired early and Ursula followed five years later, when I began to get my superannuation. We needed to be free for other commitments and, more than that, we did not feel justified in paying such large sums towards the ever-increasing military budget.

It was not until 1982 that we realised the possibility of withholding some of our income tax: that part which by now we were paying direct by cheque, under Schedule D, on a small income from rent and casual employment. Some people had already started doing it. This was a form of conscientious objection: a refusal to pay others to do what one can't do oneself. There would be no possibility for objection in nuclear war.

The general pattern of events was repeated several times: we first paid the 'legitimate' part of our income tax demand and then sent a diversionary cheque, as we call it, for the proportion of our income tax that was spent on arms. This proportion was simply the ratio of the total amount spent on arms to the total amount collected in income tax. Which is really a symbolic figure, since taxes are collected in many other ways than from income tax. It now comes to something like 52 per cent. The cheque would be made out to 'Inland Revenue: National Health Service A/c' and would usually be returned, as the Inland Revenue cannot accept any monies except those designated specifically for them. It is then distributed from what is called the Consolidated Fund to the various ministries and purposes of the government.

If the money was not sent in the ordinary way, after various warnings and Final Notices, we would be taken to the County Court, usually before a Registrar first, in private, to determine whether we had a legitimate case to go before a judge in the open court. I say 'we' because, although the earnings on which we were taxed were partly Ursula's, and I only was liable since the tax was in my name, we still considered we were in it together. In fact, Ursula was my 'Mackenzie person' at all our hearings. This is someone who can act as an adviser, but may not speak in a hearing – from the name of a person in a previous case. If the Registrar did not 'strike out' the case (which he did in our first case in 1983), it would go on to the public hearing before a County Court judge.

But in our case in 1983, when I didn't pay after the Registrar's order to do so, the Inland Revenue attempted to take the money from our bank account by what is known as 'garnishee order'. But the bank manager refused to hand over the money, since we have a joint account and the tax is in my name only.

The next step was our first visit from the bailiffs. These are officers of the County Court. They had to seize goods to a sufficient value to cover the amount I owed, plus the costs of the auction. After looking round, the chief bailiff decided to take our car. He was very pleasant to us and tried to persuade us that we had made our point and that it would be much easier for us all if we would pay up now. Ursula and I have been told a number of times that 'we have made our point', but we do not agree. We have repeatedly told the Inland Revenue that we will not willingly pay for nuclear weapons, leaving it to them to find means of collecting their taxes. As we are withholding our consent to paying, the money must be taken from us, and our point is not made if we pay voluntarily.

The auction of our small car, a Renault 4, which we share with the Quaker family next door, was interesting. On the morning of the auction I woke up thinking that we needed a handbill to give out at the auction rooms, explaining the circumstances of the sale and its significance to us and our friends next door. So I lettered and duplicated an A5 handbill, as follows:

> PAY TAXES FOR PEACE NOT WAR... Our car was taken by the bailiffs because we could not voluntarily hand over the 45 per cent of our income tax that is spent on armaments. – If we don't regain it, we shall be paying (with costs) far more than the tax we withheld. – If we *do*, it will be used communally, as before, with our friends... Arthur & Ursula Windsor.

In front of the auction rooms, where the car was on display, we handed out the handbills before the auction. I noticed a man examining the car carefully and I gave him one. He read it, paused and said: 'In that case I won't bid; I agree with what you're doing!' At noon other auction business was stopped and our auction began. Outside the auction rooms a crowd of our sympathisers with banners, and TV and radio crews were waiting, while my friend Terry Robson and I alone bid for the car. The sale was stopped by the bailiff when we reached £300.00 and the car was now technically Terry's. We got a good amount of free publicity for the cause, as TV coverage was good, both before and after the sale.

My next County Court appearance was in January 1984. The Registrar had allowed this, but the hearing was adjourned, since the Inland Revenue said they had not had sufficient time to prepare for it, although I was perfectly ready. Under a new judge, the hearing was held in February. As before, Ursula and I were helped by the support of both friends and the media, who were becoming quite friendly to us.

A crowd, some of whom had to sit on the floor, gathered in the court. Before the entry of the judge, a Friend prayed for justice. There was a hush; the atmosphere was like that in a Friends' meeting.

For these hearings, it had been agreed by war tax resisters that it would be better to be unrepresented. We were given help and good advice by the Lawyers for Nuclear Disarmament, who are working hard trying to establish that nuclear weapons, in particular, are illegal under the laws of this land, particularly the Genocide Act of 1969. I was given ample time to make my defence and to support my thesis I called, as an expert witness, a doctor who is well versed in the probable effects of nuclear war. Part of my defence stated:

> During the last war I was in the army for six years; during and after the war (especially when the atom bombs were dropped on Hiroshima and Nagasaki) I became convinced that all war was immoral. I therefore find it abhorrent to pay others to do what I am unwilling to do (i.e. bear arms). I claim the same human right of conscientious objection to *paying* for others to do military service as the British citizen has under the 1916 Act—or under Article 9 of the European Convention of Human Rights—to doing military service himself. Modern warfare is such that any future war is likely to be fought impersonally (using long-range weapons of destruction) rather than by military conscripts. So responsibility has shifted from the individual to the state. The only way I can use my own personal responsibility is by refusing (or attempting to refuse) to allow the state to use the money I contribute, to plan, prepare and wage war.

This was my basic, personal plea; there followed other objections, based on the illegality of nuclear weapons under the Genocide Act, 1969. But my main objection was a religious one:

> My main objection (which undergirds and overrides all others) is religious and moral. I have been a Christian believer as long as I can remember, and a Quaker since 1951. The Quaker Peace Testimony of 1661 says: 'The spirit of Christ, which leads us into all truth, will never move us to fight and war against any man with outward weapons, neither for the kingdom of Christ nor for the kingdoms of this world.' To Christians, the rule of love must be the guiding principle of life, especially in relationship with all human beings. Discipleship of Christ conflicts with the use of violence. The early Quaker (Fox) said '...live in the virtue of that life and power that takes away the occasion of all wars.' We should act according to the Light of Christ within, which we believe is available to all people and which shows us what is right and wrong and gives us the power to act on it. We try to live the kind of life that makes weapons unnecessary. So we still refuse to bear arms, *even*

81

in an apparently good cause, and if the moral law within us conflicts with the duty imposed by the state, 'We must obey God rather than men' (Acts 5:29). If we have to suffer for this, we must do so. For me to provide – or help to provide – weapons of mass destruction is not only in violation of our own statute law but also in violation of public morality (and I would add that British law is said to be based on Christian morality) and of my religious conviction.

I added that my objection is based not on fear of what may happen to us, but rather on the evil of our imposing such terrible casualties on others, and I continued:

Nevertheless, as a father and grandfather, I am concerned that my children and their children should live free from the threat of mass destruction and the pollution of this earth.

I also had to point out that this matter is of such vital importance to us all, and of such an exceptional nature that it cannot be argued that if my objection were allowed to stand, it would open the door to others who object to paying taxes for any other specific purpose.

But all to no avail. Although the judge listened courteously, or appeared to be listening, he made no reference to my defence when giving his judgement, but limited himself to saying that, as I had not paid the sum owing, he ordered me to do so within 14 days, failing which 'execution would be made...' and 'warrants issued for recovery of the sums stated...', etc.

Thus in July (1984) we had another visit from the bailiffs; this time they took a number of items of furniture (an antique table, a large dining-table, a bureau, with a washing-machine and other items). Terry Robson again bid for me against all comers, at the auction on 30 July. I stayed outside the auction-rooms, with the small demonstration which, as usual, was supporting us, with good media coverage as well. The antique table raised £390.00 and the auction was then stopped and the other items not sold. But owing to the fairly high price of the table, the 15 per cent that I paid the auctioneer was quite high, so that I paid (with removal costs of the furniture and court fees) about three times the amount I originally owed in tax. Of course the balance remaining, after deduction of the debt and other expenses, is returned to one in due course.

Meanwhile, the first instalment of tax for the next tax year had fallen due. I had a Registrar's hearing, which was 'struck out', against which I appealed in the County Court on 2 August. Another judge this time angrily objected to my using 'his' court as a platform for my views, adding that it was 'a matter for Parliament'; he also said something about people next trying to get out of paying for dog licences. He dismissed my appeal, but without giving me leave to appeal against *his* judgement. I had to appear before him again to ask for leave to appeal (which I knew would be refused). Such is legal procedure. As the judge was on holiday, this could not happen until 27 September, but this time the judge was unexpectedly amenable. He seemed to respect, though not agree with, our cause, though the result was the same: appeal dismissed. He said however that we could take it to the Court of Appeal, but without (he implied) much hope of success.

This I decided to do and informed the Inland Revenue that I was taking my appeal to the High Court, an involved process, which took the rest of the year, but, not through my fault, was never completed.

So it was not until the spring of 1985 that I received a Judgement Summons from the County Court. This shook us a little. The document stated that I had to satisfy the Court as to my means (to pay the amount I owed) and to give reason why I should not be sent to prison or, alternatively, be made bankrupt. Until now I had not thought of prison as a possibility, except for 'contempt of court'. I now saw that, in refusing to obey a court order to pay, I had committed contempt of court.

On the day of the hearing (12 April, 1985), before the same judge as on 22 February 1984, the court once more was crowded with supporters. The judge took it for granted that I had the means to pay and, asking about the appeal which didn't succeed, proceeded quite quickly to give his judgement. He said I must pay within three weeks or go to prison for three weeks. I told him immediately that this was pointless, as I did not intend to pay anyway. He replied that I must let him have his own opinion on that. (I thought privately that the Inland Revenue were only using prison as a threat.)

But it was rather a blow. We had expected at the most to have a one-week prison sentence. Three seemed rather harsh. However, we had always said we were willing to take whatever consequences our action might produce. I knew that Ursula was with me in this, and many other supporters were behind me. The media gave us some good publicity; the three weeks would be up on 3 May 1985, my birthday. I let slip this fact to a reporter, and we were visited at home by a TV crew who made quite a good four-minute film of us both in which we were able to state our convictions quite clearly and my confidence in the power of God to uphold me through the coming prison sentence.

I did not then know that it would be ten months before the bailiff would come for me. We lived life very fully for the next few weeks, believing that any moment my freedom would end. It was a good experience to know what it feels like to face a possible curtailment of life or freedom. Later we tended to forget it, until friends asked kindly what was happening about the prison sentence. We knew nothing; the initiative was with the Inland Revenue to apply for a 'warrant of committal'. By February 1986 we knew that it was imminent, and the last weeks were more difficult; a week or so before it actually happened we knew that the I.R. had applied for the warrant and that the bailiff (who has powers of arrest) could come any day. When he finally came, at noon on 6 March, Ursula greeted him with the words: 'Thank goodness you've come!' The bailiff, who had taken our car and our furniture previously, and who had always been very civil to us, now seemed even more sympathetic to our cause. He assured us that prison was not 'the end'. As he went out of the front door with me, he turned round and said: 'Law is not the same thing as justice.'

He took me to the prison in his private car; the whole process, from then on, seemed something dream-like to me. For Ursula, a time of intense, often tiring, activity was beginning. She immediately had an interview with the local radio. After I had been given a fairly good lunch, by myself in a very bare cell, I went through the 'Reception' process: particulars taken, property removed, stripped, given a bath and prison uniform. As I was coming from the bathroom, which was next to the Reception office, and was being given clothes, I heard the 1 o'clock news on the local radio coming from the office. This was followed by Ursula's voice speaking of my incarceration and the reasons for it. This was Reception indeed for me.

I was given a cell by myself to start with. It was 6 March and rather cold in this end cell, with two outer walls. I had to ask for an extra blanket after the first night. But after three days I was put into a cell with one other inmate; I was lucky, as most cells contain three prisoners. Ted was an older man, nearer my own age, and we got on well together, doing crossword puzzles and listening to plays and light music (not pop) on the radio together.

Prison life is very much like army life; if you are prepared to knuckle under and be a nonentity, while at the same time quite aware of what you can do and get, then you survive quite well. There is, of course, a negative side to it. The general feeling of oppression and an overall futility were to me little different from the feeling I had in 1940 in my earlier months in the army. There is the same necessity to obey shouted orders, to 'keep one's nose clean', to find out the best way and when to do certain things (one is never actually told), and the superficial bonhomie. Then there is 'slopping out': some people find this degrading. To me however it is a natural act; as a child I was used to the chamber-pot or pail in the bedroom, since there was no bathroom. This had to be emptied next morning in the outside lavatory, round at the back of the scullery. It was no worse in prison. At least one didn't have to go out in the rain. The plastic bucket might stink when emptied, but it had a lid which covered it tightly at other times.

Everyone had assumed that I should get a week's remission and 'do' only two weeks instead of three. On the morning after I got there, I found that as a Civil Prisoner I would get no remission, and would have to serve the full term of three weeks. But on the other hand I had the privilege of a visit (of 15 to 20 minutes) every day except Sunday. The Prison Chaplain informed Ursula of these two facts on the same morning as I knew them, and she was there in the afternoon visiting me, with two friends; and every time (except one) she came with different people to visit me, so quite a number of people now have a slight taste of what it is like within the prison walls. On the subject of the length of my sentence: when I think of the Plowshares protesters in the USA, with sentences of 12 or 18 *years*, I feel very humble and cannot regard my three weeks as much of a sacrifice.

I found the other prisoners usually pleasant and helpful. The main time of contact is during the one hour's daily exercise in the prison yard, when one can meet people from other landings or wings from one's own. Other times are when fetching meals from the kitchen or at work. As we circulated monotonously around the yard, I found that small knots of two and three prisoners would form and reform. In this way I got to know a few of the prisoners. One or two people approached me eagerly, when I first arrived, knowing why I was there, and expressing their agreement with my position on arms. Some, including one prison officer, debated the question with me: a worthwhile side of my prison sentence.

There were P., the young man sentenced to 15 years for robbing Post Offices; and K., from Zimbabwe, who had been caught by the customs people receiving a packet of cannabis and who later became prison librarian; and the man from Hereford who boasted of stealing a video set, worth £100 on the market, every day. These were all nice chaps and I found it mystifying that they had knowingly embarked on these crimes (except for K., who maintained that cannabis should be made legal). It seemed that a large proportion of prisoners were there for burglary; one I talked to seemed to have little idea of the havoc that burglaries can make in ordinary people's lives.

One of the features of prison life that I found hardest was the well-known attitude of the majority to the sex offenders, who can invoke 'Rule 43' and are then put (at Gloucester Prison) in 'C' Wing for their own protection. It seems to be a prison convention that one has to hate these people with a murderous hatred. I had a discussion about this with an apparently reasonable young man (in prison for 'GBH', that is for inflicting 'grievous bodily harm', when the worse for drink). I expressed my view that the sex offenders should be given treatment, while he told me graphically of all the terrible acts they were known to have committed. In the end, he stopped the conversation, on the grounds that he felt so strongly about it that he couldn't go on. About a week before my release I read in *The Guardian* that a probation officer, Ray Wyre, at Albany Prison, on the Isle of Wight, has started an enlightened programme of help for sex offenders, to encourage them to face their problems and when they return to life 'outside' not to continue to offend in the same way, as so often happens.

I have always been a fairly solitary person, as far as family life would allow; it was therefore not so bad when I was in a cell by myself for three days, or when I had to be 'banged up' by myself, when Ted was working and I not. When I entered the prison, the few items of my own property that I was allowed to keep were my watch, a biro, the *Epistles* of George Fox, *Moby Dick* (which I had decided to read at last now that I had time), and some daily readings by Bishop George Appleton that I had photocopied from a book, from which Ursula would also be reading each day. I read solidly from the books for the first two or three days. My Bible had been taken from me, but the Chaplain brought me one on the second day; I sometimes read from that also. I obtained an exercise book from the Education office; the following are some notes I made during the first few days:

6.3.86 (Day of admission): Read Epistle 16 (Fox). V. helpful today. (An extract from the Epistle reads: 'Wait upon God in that which is pure... and stand still in it everyone, to see your Saviour, to make you free from that which the Light doth discover to you to be evil. For the voice of the Bridegroom is heard in the land; and Christ is come among the prisoners, to visit them in the prison-houses; they have all hopes of releasement and free pardon, and to come out freely for the debt is paid; wait for the manifestation of it, and he that comes out of prison shall reign.')

8.3.86 (Sat.): Up ½ hr. later — Ep. 24 'learn... *to be low and meek in heart... they that wait upon the Lord, he will give them their heart's desire.*' (G.F's emphases). What is my heart's desire? At the moment: that U. should be upheld by the Lord and not be downcast at my 21 days! — I didn't quite realise before, what it was I had to be fortified against. — 'Though you have not a foot of ground to stand upon, yet you have the power of God to skip and leap in.' (These words of Fox's to Friends under persecution had been a great help to us throughout the Court hearings and in the months leading up to this time itself.)

13.3.86 (Bible reading) 1Thess. 3:12 — 'And the Lord make you to increase & abound in love one toward another, & toward all men, even as we do toward you.'
W.G.'s card (same date):
   'We are they who will not take
   From palace, priest or code
   A meaner law than brotherhood,
   A lower Lord than God.'

18.3.86 (Radio 4 Service) Mother Teresa's prayer: 'Make us worthy, Lord, to serve our fellow men.'

These are some notes from my book; there is also, on a different page, a quotation from a greeting card from a stranger of Worcester:

17.3.86: 'You are never given a wish without also being given the power to make it true. You may have to work for it, however. Millions of us share the same wish — Close your eyes and feel the support.' R.B.

This strikes me as similar to George Fox, when he talks of God's giving 'them their heart's desire'.

I have mentioned my mail. Let me quote from what Ursula has written on this subject:

I felt sure the day would come when Arthur would feel down-hearted, but long before that could happen the mail started to arrive: 20, 40, 70 letters and cards a day! The prison authorities could not hope to get through all those every day, and just a few of them remained unopened until he got home, but all the rest of the 500-odd Arthur was able to read in his cell, often till late at night, because in the morning he had to give them up, so that they could be put with his belongings for the day of his release. This was the only way, apparently, the prison authorities could cope with this flow of correspondence. The volume and contents of the mail from literally all over the country, many of them strangers, as well as from relatives, friends and Friends abroad, many times moved us both to tears, and we experienced something of the upholding power of prayer. In addition we were excited by the positive effect our action was having on many people who felt spurred on to further work for peace. We were asked many times whether it was all worthwhile, and this was surely the answer.

The latter point is well made in a very moving letter I received from a stranger in a village near Lancaster, of which I give an extract:

Dear Mr. Windsor,
... I saw your case reported on the news last weekend, and I felt I had to offer you my support...

Whilst it is obvious you believe deeply about the horrors of any future wars, it is still a brave action you have taken. May I thank you for further highlighting to blind politicians the stupidity and futility of their actions. I am sure it has made other parents like me think again about what we let them do in the name of defence.

I am a 39-year-old parent of three young children, and I joined CND with my wife a couple of years ago. What made me take this small step by your standards was the feeling that as I looked in on them before I went to bed and as I kissed them goodnight, I could not imagine that they had better than a 50/50 chance of dying of old age on our planet. That was the turning point for me...

We are considering forming our own Christian CND group here in our village, prompted by your protest. I am sure you will have considered it all worthwhile in the end, but I would just like you to know that it has been seen as a wonderful gesture by us and our thoughts and prayers are with you.

Best Wishes
T.S.(signed)

This letter was representative of many I received; during the first days that I began to receive cards and letters, I began to put them up (in the only make-shift way I could) on the wall-board provided in the cell. Many were beautiful, or moving or humorous; R.F., who had been in Gloucester prison himself for wire-cutting at Molesworth, sent a card with a quote (adapted) from Thoreau: 'In an unjust society, the only place for a just person is in prison.' There were many cards drawn or painted by children, which moved me greatly. This was something that gave me great support, added to my knowledge that many people were praying for me. At one visit I told Ursula I was 'walking on air'.

Several friends subscribed to send me flowers by Interflora (partly to test whether this was possible for men, as it is for women in prison), and the Governor, with my consent, finally had them put into the chapel, where all could see them—though very few knew where they had come from. I saw them two or three times.

For her part, Ursula has said of her life at the time:

> My life outside was, of course, very different and more difficult to describe, but it was an exciting as well as exhausting time. Many times I thought I had come to the end, when I knew there was more to do, and always I was given strength to do it.

But for me she was a great support, coming practically every day to see me, sending the *Guardian* and *Observer* and (after some red tape) a transistor radio—which we were allowed to have, providing it had no VHF band.

The day of my release, 26 March, was a memorable one for all of us. For me, I went through the routine of release fairly quickly and emerged from the front door of the prison by 7.30 a.m., to a cheer from about sixty supporters and hugs from Ursula and others. There was an array of television and press people in front and also Dennis Canavan MP, who had come down from London very early to greet me. We had to give some interviews and then went home for a breakfast of hot-cross buns and coffee. Dennis Canavan and Dave Ford (of the Peace Tax Campaign) then drove back to London, where Ursula and I later joined them in the House of Commons for lunch. On the train journey, Ursula and I had time to get acquainted again after the separation; during the visits to the prison we had never been alone. After lunch we were joined by Gerald Drewett, chairman of the Peace Tax Campaign, for a press conference, which gave us a foretaste of Dennis Canavan's skilful handling of his Peace Tax Bill, which he introduced in the Commons that afternoon, under the 'Ten Minute Rule'. We listened from the Strangers' Gallery. His coverage of the subject in so short a time was impressive, and the way he supported his plea for a Peace Tax Fund by my recent prison experience was moving for us. Having reached its first reading, the Bill cannot now get a second, but a good deal of publicity has been achieved, as it has been published in Hansard and printed.

A further development has been the tabling of a Motion for a Resolution in the European Parliament by six British MEPs ('tabled by Mr HINDLEY, Mr FALCONER, Mr BALFE, Mr CRYER, Mr NEWMAN and Ms TONGUE'), and as the motion states:

...pursuant to Rule 47 of the Rules of Procedure on the gaol sentence of Mr Arthur WINDSOR

The European Parliament

- noting that Mr Arthur WINDSOR, 69 years of age, was gaoled at Gloucester, UK, on 6 March 1986, for refusing to pay taxes towards the purchase of weapons,
- noting that Mr WINDSOR has paid the non-defence part of his taxes in the normal way and has repeatedly tried to pay the defence part of his taxes to various institutions in order to ensure that none of his money was allocated to defence-spending,
- noting that this is the first gaoling of a conscientious objector in the UK since the abolition of conscription,
- noting that conscientious objection is recognised as a basic human right in many countries,

1. Condemns the gaoling of Mr WINDSOR;
2. Calls for all Member States to extend to conscientious objectors to taxes for military purposes the same rights as to conscientious objectors to actual military service;
3. Calls upon its relevant committee to include this matter in the report it is currently preparing on conscientious objection.

It is good that the question of conscientious objection to taxes for 'military purposes' should be associated with the whole question of conscientious objection itself, which is exercising the European Parliament at the moment.

A television interviewer once asked me: 'What do you answer when your critics say that by your action you have put an unfair burden on the tax-payer?', who (he meant) has to pay a large sum for one's keep in prison for three weeks: plus or minus £900. This question took my breath away; was it *my* action that took me to prison? Ursula and I, by withholding part of our tax (that not used for peaceful purposes), had, step by step, via a number of hardships, arrived (almost imperceptibly to us) at the place where the *Inland Revenue* took this action against us. So I went to prison. To many this must have seemed like a humiliating hardship and I don't want to deny its negative side. But, as I have tried to say, I have felt such an effect, a warmth of loving support, together with what I believe to be the upholding power of prayer, that I came through it unharmed, and humbler and wiser, I hope. Ursula and I feel now, as much as ever, that it is required of us to continue with this kind of witness, whatever the future may hold.

Equally, this experience has shown how following the light in one's conscience can encourage others to do whatever they can, for God, for the cause of peace and justice, and for human rights and freedom of conscience.

To quote George Fox again:

> Though you have not a foot of ground to stand upon, yet you have the power of God to skip and leap in; standing in that, which is your life, that is everlasting. (Epistle 206).

CHAPTER TEN

The Turkish Peace Association

DORA KALKAN

Dora Kalkan is Turkish, and a member of the Turkish Peace Association. In order to put Dora's account into the context of recent Turkish history, we have prefaced her chapter with a brief review of the significant events that have occurred in Turkey since the formation of the TPA.

The Turkish Peace Association was formed by a group of intellectuals, writers, lawyers, doctors, engineers, educationalists, and other leading members of Turkish society on 3 April 1977. Its President, Mahmut Dikerdem, had been a diplomat for forty years, an ambassador, a lecturer in International Law, and the author of two books on the Third World. At its height, the TPA had 350 members, a large executive committee, and a strong voice in public debate over Turkey's role in the modern world. The TPA was legally active for three and a half years until the coup which brought a group of right-wing army generals to power on 12 September 1980. On the same day, the TPA was declared illegal, its offices were ransacked, and all its documents confiscated.

The founding conference of the Turkish Peace Association in April 1977 had adopted the following aims:

— The abolition of nuclear weapons and all weapons of mass destruction; an end to the arms race; the dissolution of all military alliances; the removal from all countries of foreign bases and foreign troops.

— An end to the use of force in international disputes, and a commitment to resolving them by negotiation.

92

- Peaceful co-existence between nations with different political systems; rejection of interference in the internal affairs of other nations; respect for the independence and sovereignty of nations.

- The development of economic and cultural ties between nations within a framework of friendship and mutually beneficial co-operation.

- An immediate end to all forms of racism and colonialism.

- The re-allocation of the enormous funds reserved for armaments to the eradication of disease and human misery.

- Respect for human rights; the possession and control by the people of their national resources, and the freedom of the people to determine, according to forms chosen by themselves, social and economic reforms.

- The implementation of United Nations resolutions concerning matters of peace and security.

These aims corresponded both with the revival of peace movements all over the world, and with the specific struggles within Turkey for peace and democracy. They brought the Turkish Peace Association into direct conflict with the army junta led by Kenan Evren, and harassment and interrogation of TPA members began immediately after the coup. In February 1982 the President of the TPA, Mahmut Dikerdem, and the Executive were arrested in a dawn raid. They were taken to a special detention centre of the Istanbul Second Armoured Command, and detained in grossly overcrowded cells with no heating, no ventilation, and no windows. Despite strong protests from the EEC Council of Ministers at this time, the TPA members remained confined in brutal and degrading conditions for nine months, at which time they were unexpectedly granted bail. During this nine-month period of internment, Mahmut Dikerdem was refused medical treatment for the prostatic cancer from which he was suffering.

In May 1982 the indictment against the Turkish Peace Association was prepared. In the words of the military prosecutor: 'The TPA has continually opposed bilateral defence treaties to which Turkey is a party, military bases, and NATO, and has accordingly tried to form public opinion in this direction. ...The TPA has become a secret organisation to undermine the authority of State and Government and to cause the breakdown of order in the nation.' During the course of the trial (which lasted until November 1983), the presiding judge insisted that Peter the Great's last will and testament (dated 1725!) be read out in court to show that the TPA had 'aided Russian designs' by criticising NATO. The judge maintained that since the United Nations 'New International Economic Order' was a code-word for 'Soviet-style planning', a TPA seminar on this subject was an indication of its 'intent to subvert'. It was alleged that the TPA's use of the word 'peace' was a 'code-name for communism'. Lawyers for the defence were severely restricted in the presentation of their case. In November 1983, less than one week after 'elections' had heralded the 'return to democracy', the TPA members were given savage prison sentences, and taken to a military prison.

On 27 September 1984 a new peace trial opened. In the 'Peace II' trial, 48 active members of the Turkish Peace Association were tried with charges identical to those made against the TPA Executive in the first trial. Among defendants in the second rial were fifteen lawyers, four doctors, seven writers, six actors, two former members of parliament, three leaders of chambers of engineering, three professors, two union leaders, three journalists, and three former TV news broadcasters.

In his final statement at his trial in 1983, Mahmut Dikerdem said,

> I sincerely believe that if my life's work has provided a modest service to my people, the people of Turkey who have nurtured me and to whom I owe my very being, this will be due more to three and a half years as the President of the Peace Association than my forty-year long career ... I want it to be recorded before history and world public opinion that our country's commitment to a just and lasting world peace is not merely a cliché repeated in public statements, but a cherished ideal rooted in public consciousness...

Dora Kalkan now tells her own story:

I am a medical doctor. On Tuesday 19 October 1982 at 3 p.m., two men in plain clothes knocked at the door of the room where I was doing my outpatients' clinic. They came in and abruptly told me to follow them. I was surprised, I could not understand. They held my shoulders and said, 'We are the political police. We are arresting you. You have to come with us this moment. If you make any fuss or if you try to let anybody know, you will suffer for it'.

I knew what had been going on in Turkey since the military coup on 12 September 1980. I had heard that many people had disappeared at the hands of the secret police. But I had no choice. If I had resisted, or tried to tell others in the university hospital where I was working, I knew that I and my family would suffer.

I left my room without telling anybody, and followed them into the car. The moment I stepped into the car, I was handcuffed and blindfolded. This moment was the beginning of a long, very dark period in my life. The political police took me to the police station, where I spent the night in a cell measuring one square metre. I was alone; I didn't know what was going on. I was afraid of the noises I could hear around me.

The next day I was taken to Metris Military Prison, which is situated outside Istanbul. Metris is a modern prison for political prisoners, built in 1980 according to US prison standards. It is made of iron and steel, and its aim is to break a person morally. In 1982 there were 1300 men and 200 women imprisoned there.

I was put in a small cell measuring 4 x 5 x 3 metres. There were fourteen inmates in the cell, all of us prisoners of conscience. We were two doctors, three lawyers, two civil engineers, one painter, one journalist, two students, and three housewives. Like me, most of the inmates did not know why they had been imprisoned.

For the first three weeks my family did not know where I was. They had to search at the hospitals and the police station to find out where I had been taken. At the end of the third week, my family learned by coincidence that I was alive but imprisoned. Then they began the task of finding out why I had been arrested. For the first six months of my imprisonment I had no clue as to the charges against me. Nobody seemed to know why I was there.

On 16 March 1983, I was summoned by the Prosecutor for interrogation. This was the first time since the day of my arrest on 19 October 1982 that I had been seen by an official. The Prosecutor seemed to know a lot about my family, my career in the university, my husband and child too. The main thing he wanted to know was how I had been introduced to the idea of peace. He also insisted that I usually used the word *peace* to mean *communism*. He was extremely rude and abusive to me, insulting me on several occasions. He asked me incongruous and meaningless questions, and threatened to keep me in prison for the rest of my life. He wanted me to tell him the names of people who worked for peace.

My life in Metris Military Prison was just terrible. The cell was very small. There were twelve beds for fourteen people. We shared the beds, blankets, clothes, and every other thing. There was no space to take even two steps in the cell. Our only activity was to lie on our beds. We were permitted to go out of the cell only after the strictest strip-search. We were allowed out three times a week for only 40 minutes, when we were taken to a concrete courtyard ten metres long, where we could pace up and down. This yard was surrounded by very thick and high walls. The only thing which could actually be seen was the sky.

Only close relatives were allowed to visit us, for ten minutes once a week. This is how the interview took place. The prisoner was strip-searched and then taken by two young soldiers to a small glass cell measuring one square metre. In front of the cell was another glass cell one metre away, where the relatives (in my case my father and mother) would enter. They would have two young soldiers with them. There were earphones in the cells. These were used by the soldiers and prisoner. The conversation could take place only in Turkish, and only for ten minutes. The soldiers had the right to stop the conversation at any time. If they suspected a forbidden topic (for example, asking questions or giving information about prison conditions), they would stop the interview. Interviews with lawyers took place in exactly the same way. There could be no private conversation between the lawyer and the defendant.

The food in the prison was of the worst possible quality. It was very scarce, too. We were given only beans, peas, macaroni and bread. There were no fresh vegetables or fruit. There was no meat or any kind of animal protein. There was no real fibre. Food was sometimes used as a means of punishment. On one of the holidays a very palatable-looking dish of beans was brought to the cell. When we tasted it, we realised that it was so salty we could never eat it. We washed it, but it was not possible to get rid of the salt. We could not eat it. On another occasion when food was given to prisoners it contained so much pepper that nobody could eat it.

We had no contact with the outside world. There was no radio or television; no newspapers or journals. Even my medical books were confiscated and never given back, on the pretext that they contained subversive ideas against the interests of the State.

We had no paper or pencil. We were given two sheets of paper each week in order to write two letters. We gave the letters to the policewomen, who read and photocopied them. Letters took three or four months to arrive at their destinations, and we had to wait three to five months for the replies.

We were forbidden to have any verbal communication with any of the inmates in the other cells. We were not supposed to smile, wave, or say hello to the policewomen or any other official who entered our cells for official weekly searches. We were kept in complete isolation, with no physical activity, insufficient food, and no contact with the outside world. Many inmates lost weight, many were in need of medical treatment, especially the ones who were brought from the police station, where they had been severely tortured. There were pregnant women who were not taken to see doctors. There were sick women and even women suffering from cancer who were left to die.

On 14 August 1983 the prison authorities brought specially trained teams to search the cells. They suspected that prisoners were communicating with each other, that they were studying socialism, and that topics like freedom, democracy, and peace were being discussed. The teams entered our cells after we had been taken to dungeons. Ten hours later when we returned to our cells, we could not believe our eyes. All our clothes, sheets, and pillow cases, were torn to strips. Our mattresses were torn to pieces. All the food was thrown into the toilet. Pictures had been stabbed, especially at the genitals. The iron beds were unscrewed to see if anything was concealed inside them. Every piece of paper in the cell was confiscated. We had nowhere to sleep and nowhere to sit but the concrete floor.

These things happened. We had no means of complaining. We were left to the mercy of the military authorities.

I remained in prison until 8 October 1983, when I was released on bail.

In March 1986 all TPA members were released from prison on bail, pending a retrial of those sentenced in the 'Peace 1' trial. However, in 1987, all charges were dropped against the TPA defendants as Turkey, under pressure from Western European governments and non-government groups, continued to move towards greater democracy. However Dora Kalkan does not plan to return to Turkey at present. Her knowledge that nearly two thousand people died in prisons during the rule of the military junta, and that many of them were prisoners of conscience, makes her wary.

CHAPTER ELEVEN

'Free to Act With Integrity'

JENNIFER HAINES

Jennifer Haines, a graduate in Zoology, and with a Master's degree in elementary education, started her professional career as a teacher before taking up social work in Philadelphia and Washington DC. While in Washington she was arrested twice for her witness against a trade fair concerned with promoting arms sales. For the last six years she has lived in Denver, Colorado where her repeated prayerful trespasses at the Rocky Flats Nuclear Weapons plant have led to frequent arrests and terms of imprisonment.

I call myself a monk.

'A monk? But you're a woman.'

Yes, but 'nun' doesn't suggest my vocation to contemplative prayer, and, besides, I'm not officially a member of any church. I grew up Quaker in the eastern United States (which means that I grew up pacifist); I embraced Christianity with protestant charismatics; and I worship now mostly with Catholics. I'm at home with mystics of any faith. Sometimes I think I must be a hermit, but for many years now, pretty much since I graduated from college in the late 1960s, I've felt called to live in inner cities.

'In all that noise and pollution? Why don't you find yourself a nice cabin in a lonely mountainside?'

Believe me, I'd rather, but God says, 'No.' I know why. There's so much woundedness in cities, so much need for prayer. I've been connected for several years with the Catholic Worker community in

Denver, which follows Christ's call to feed the hungry and shelter the homeless, and my centeredness in prayer — such as it is — seems to be something of a refuge for them.

'I don't understand. What do you *do*?'

I try not to do anything. I try to be quiet and to let God's love for me and in me and through me reach out to the world. I do love people a lot. One of the places where I seem to need to pray a great deal is the nuclear weapons plant outside Denver — Rocky Flats. I try to stand with God there, who loves all those 'defence' workers infinitely, and to whom weapons of mass destruction are anathema. I hurt with God over our inhumanity to each other and our willingness to destroy each other because we don't trust God enough to know that we're secure in God's love and don't have to be afraid of anything.

Sometimes I pray outside the gate, where I can greet the workers and make friends with them. And sometimes I step across the line that the US government says marks 'their' property. I say the property is God's, and that no one has a right to use it for building nuclear weapons. I need to stand there on God's behalf, claiming God's sovereignty. When I do that, I get arrested and charged with trespassing.

'Oh well, trespassing isn't serious.'

Perhaps not. At most, it's a misdemeanor. But if you cross a 'barrier' — and Rocky Flats has erected a symbolic little knee-high gate that's closed across the access road only when folks are 'protesting' out there — you can be sentenced to up to a year in prison and/or a $5,000 fine. And when I first came to Rocky Flats in 1981, there was a court injunction against trespassing, which meant that you could get the maximum, for contempt of court, even if you *didn't* cross a 'barrier'.

I've been arrested there six times. Each time, I learn a little more about my relationship to the society — and to its political, economic, legal, and penal systems — that I grew up with. I've learned that I have infinite freedom in God to choose to do right, regardless of what's being done around me or what's being asked of me. My own integrity and attempted faithfulness to God require that I not participate in what I believe is wrong or incompatible with God's reign of love. I'm not trying to change the world, only to live the Gospel. And as I grow in experience, I find that there's less and less of the way the systems work that I'm willing to participate in.

So, by the time I went out to Rocky Flats to pray on Christmas morning, 1984, I already knew that an adversary legal system, based on each party attempting to get the most it can for itself with no regard for truth, has nothing to do with loving one's neighbour and seeking justice. I will have nothing to do with it, beyond walking where I'm escorted and responding courteously and caringly to persons. I will not plead. I will not accept legal help. I will not present any kind of 'defence'. I will not make any kind of promise to return to court, and I will not return voluntarily. I do not consider any order of the court binding on my choices. I will not pay a fine, accept a court assignment to community service, or co-operate with probation. Whatever the court may do to me about which I have no choice, I live with.

By Christmas morning, 1984, I had already been held in quite a number of county jails and been sent to federal prison once. I knew that I was as free inside as out. I do not believe that jails or prisons should exist at all, and I'm not willing to assist in their functioning. I will not work for them or provide information for them or accept their authority as higher than that of God or my own conscience. I will not obey any order that I do not consider inherently reasonable. I had been punished a lot — isolated, denied 'privileges' (such as visits), transferred — but my freedom to act with integrity had not been suppressed.

And I had had a lot of wonderful experiences of loving people in the system, developing relationships with them, and seeing them step outside of the system's own rules and expectations in response to me and my insistence on my values.

I did not go to Rocky Flats on Christmas morning, 1984, planning to step across the line. I often don't plan. I went thinking that the time might be right, and waiting for what God might have to say to me about it. I didn't hear God say a thing. But I finally realised that, whatever God might need for me to do, *I* needed to step across that line. I couldn't just turn around and go home. So I stepped across it. I was immediately arrested and transported to Denver City Jail. And in jail I was overwhelmed by a tremendous sense of peace, freedom, joy, and rightness, that carried me for many months. Another step in my journey with God had begun.

Federal criminal cases in the USA go first to a magistrate, who sets bond. Since I've been in Denver, I've always refused any kind of bond, including personal recognisance. So I've done a fair amount of pre-trial time in jail. The third time I came before the magistrate here, he amazed us all by releasing me without any promise to return to court. That was when I had to figure out my position on returning voluntarily. I tried it, felt compromised by it, and decided never to do it again. I was rearrested on my first non-appearance and incarcerated. But the fifth time I saw the same magistrate, he again amazed us by releasing me without a promise. That time, when the judge had me rearrested and I told her that, because I had co-defendants, I *did* intend to come to the trial, but still couldn't promise, she also released me.

Now I had a new magistrate, new to me and new to the bench. I was (again) certain that he would keep me in custody. He did, for three days. Then he called me back, and he, too, released me without a promise to return – warning me that, if I didn't, I could expect a year in prison for contempt of court. I wrote to him afterwards, as I always do, explaining my position and my understanding of his. He honored me with a personal response, clearly expressing his concern for me, and offering to find a personal friend who could discuss my position with me, hoping I would change it. His friend and I met for hot chocolate and a lovely chat. Of course, I didn't return. The judge had me rearrested and incarcerated, but he ignored the contempt of court.

It felt providential to me that I'd been assigned to this judge. Assignments are presumably random, among five or six federal judges. I had had the same one four times, developing such a sense of personal relationship with her that, when she released me without a promise to show up for trial, and then left me at large without even an *indication* that I would show up for sentencing (my letter to her had clearly suggested otherwise) and had me rearrested when I didn't, she felt she had to punish me for my contempt of court twice in the same case, but apparently couldn't bring herself to give me more than an utterly token five days in jail. She even told a newspaper reporter (of all people), 'I like Jennifer'. I like her, too. I wouldn't think of holding against her the fact that she once sent me to prison. One can expect such things of judges.

The judge I had this time was new to me, but he had sentenced a friend of mine a year earlier for exactly the same thing I did – stepping across that little gate on Christmas day – and had been very harsh. He gave my friend a choice between a year in prison and paying *restitution* to Rocky Flats – an unbelievably punishing choice, since my friend wasn't ready for prison. I was, and I wanted the judge to know that his sentence wasn't a deterrent to witness for peace. My coming before him the following year said as much in itself.

Because I refuse to participate in the legal process, my trials are boring. The prosecutor and judge insist that the only issue is a straightforward one of trespass, which is easy to prove. I don't object to anything. If at the end I feel I have anything to say, I say it at the time of closing arguments. I have nothing to defend, nothing to prove, nothing to accomplish. I did what I needed to do at Rocky Flats. I don't really care what the court does. I've discovered that such goalless attitude frees me up immeasurably to love the judge and anyone else who might think of me as an adversary. I think of them as friends. It's occurred to me that this choice to receive everyone as a friend is essentially all there is to disarmament.

At sentencing, I made a statement: I said that I had appreciated what opportunity there had been for dialogue with the jury and judge, and hoped for more.

'Frankly,' said the judge, 'I don't.'

He seems to have taken one good look at my record and decided (correctly) that I was undeterrable. Or else, perhaps, he felt it was time to teach me a lesson. On my first conviction, I had received probation. 'I don't care whether you want to co-operate or not', said the judge. 'I'm *sentencing* you to it.' On my second, including violation of the probation, I'd been given ten months in prison, later modified, entirely at the judge's initiative, to six; on my third, a fine, suspended on the condition that I not be convicted of the same thing within six months; on my fourth, including violation of the condition, a fine, suspended with no conditions. By this time, the court injunction against trespassing had been rescinded, and I had not yet stepped across a barrier, so the charge was a petty one, not carrying prison time, and I had done pre-trial time in jail. The sentence was equivalent to time served. On my fifth conviction, I was sentenced to a fine, which, of course, it was known I wouldn't pay. The federal government seems, so far, to be continuing indefinitely to try to collect unpaid fines. In my case, I'm such a pauper that they hardly even try. I have no assets and no income. I've been living for years on love and providence. At this, my sixth sentencing, the judge skipped most of his lecture and gave me the full year.

'How do you do a year in prison?'

One day at a time. You automatically get two months of 'statutory good time' credited to the end of a one-year federal sentence, and you can earn another month of 'meritorious good time' by working. All federal prisoners are required to work. You aren't eligible for parole unless your sentence is longer than a year. So you would normally expect to do nine months on a year. I expect to do a year. I won't work, and one of the punishments for rule infractions is loss of 'good' time. So I'm prepared to lose it. I'm also prepared to do my time in solitary and to be transferred from prison to prison. That's about all they can do to me, legally.

The hardest part is the travelling. The US marshals have an airlift for transporting federal prisoners, which shuttles back and forth across the country picking you up and dropping you off at the marshals' convenience. You lay over in county jails. The process normally takes weeks. When I went to Pleasanton (near San Francisco), I was held for two weeks four hundred miles out of the way in Los Angeles. This time, I was sent to Fort Worth, Texas, which always means a layover in Oklahoma City, the worst county jail I've experienced yet. Women are crowded into a steel and concrete box just about big enough for six double bunks, a long metal table with benches, two toilets, a laundry tub, and a shower stall. The highest the population got while I was there was 16. I've talked with someone who was there when it was 22. You never leave the room. Food is pushed in through a slit in the wall. There are no windows and no natural light. One incandescent bulb gives enough light in some parts of the room to read by. There's nothing worth reading except a Bible. There's a radio. No place to exercise. Precious little in the way of vitamins, and wholly inadequate medical care. Women who've travelled with the marshals are generally thrilled to get to prison.

If you have to do time in the United States, the best place to do it is in federal prison. Basic living conditions in the ones I've seen — light, warmth, sanitation, nutrition, exercise — are acceptable, even in detention. If you go along with the rules and do what you're told, you can lead an almost normal life in some respects — work, recreation, social life, religious services, celebrations. But you never forget, and the system doesn't let you forget, that you're a prisoner, a second-class citizen (if citizen at all), a piece of federal property, an object, a number. The level of consent, of submission to prison authority, that's required to stay in the general population is beyond me. And in detention you have to struggle with being forgotten and ignored and simply not noticed so much that you can begin to wonder if you're a person at all, if you have an identity, if you exist. Feelings about that began to get to me after six months or so. A challenge to spiritual growth.

My first federal prison had been Pleasanton. I made it through the intake process there and spent one night on the compound before I first refused to work and was locked down. That's about all I saw of Pleasanton. I was immediately sentenced by the prison 'disciplinary' committee to a transfer, even though the 'offence' wasn't serious. My refusal to be cowed by prison authority is *very* threatening to prison personnel. Because its detenion unit was crowded, Pleasanton housed me for four of my six weeks awaiting transfer at a nearby county jail, which kept me in isolation because of my refusal to give information upon arrival. My experience is that people who expect to be obeyed come on heavily in the beginning with threats, and occasionally follow through on them. I was transferred to a Metropolitan Correctional Center (a federal institution which is like a county jail) in San Diego, California, where I was kept locked down for most of my time because of my continuing refusal to work.

At Fort Worth, I never made it out of R & D (Receiving and Discharge). I had been there less than an hour, and all I did was to refuse the background information that goes on the fingerprint card, before I was escorted directly to solitary. 'So much', I thought, 'for Fort Worth.' It's a good thing that I do fairly well in solitary. It's a natural place for prayer. You're allowed to read and write. I must admit that I love being separated from media noise and cigarette smoke. What I miss the most is nature, and being able to look out a window helps a lot. There's even some limited outdoor recreation in an enclosed yard.

But Fort Worth wasn't done with me. After a couple of days, a lieutenant came by to say that I just needed to tell them enough that they'd know I'd be safe in the general population. A little while later, the captain came. I often get visits from prison big-wigs. They want me to change, and they'll try anything—threats, punishment, reason, persuasion, enticement. I'm not quite sure who was responsible, but my mail at Fort Worth was being returned to the senders for nearly a month, and mail is a *right*, not a privilege. I also couldn't send mail out, because I didn't have money for stamps, and I worried about my

friends and family worrying about me. Fortunately, I had some access
to a telephone. But, ultimately, I have to be willing to do without
anything that might be denied me, legally or illegally, because I'm
not willing to be changed, or to respond in anger, or to sneak around
the rules, or to use the prison's grievance procedure (which I don't
respect) to try to get what I might need. I attempt to choose not to
need it. Then I'm free, free to act with integrity, and free to love – to
be who I am in God.

I didn't change, and after about three weeks, I was simply
released into the general population. I was very shortly sent back to
R & D, refused the same information, and was escorted straight back
to detention, this time with an incident report for refusing an order.
'This is it', I thought. But no: the 'disciplinary' committee threatened
a transfer, but actually sentenced me only to some punishment time
in solitary (before, I had been locked down administratively; on
punishment status, you're denied some privileges, notably, for me,
the telephone) and the loss of some 'good' days. I was out on the
compound again in time for my birthday and Easter, which was a
gift indeed.

There followed a whole series of lock-ups and releases. The
detention staff began to joke about my returning 'home'. Both
inmates and officers began to welcome me onto the compound with
compliments and good wishes. I began to feel that I was developing
some level of understanding with the captain, who chaired the 'disciplinary' committee. I had two wonderfully supportive staff people on my
living unit who tried to keep me from getting into trouble for refusing
to work. The issue didn't come up immediately, because you spend
your first week there in 'orientation'. I dutifully attended orientation
sessions when I was free to. My guiding principle is that I co-operate
with everything I possibly can, and don't refuse until I have to.

When I *was* given a job assignment, it was on the unit. The
first time I refused to do it, I thought, 'This is it'. But no: the
officer called me back to say, essentially, that he wouldn't notice
whether I did it or not. That lasted until, I think, a jealous inmate
put a bug in someone else's ear. I did get locked up for refusing,
and sentenced to a transfer. And then I got locked up for refusing
to be tested for drugs. (I never take drugs, and I know, whether they
do or not, that they can trust my word.) I was finally shipped out of
Fort Worth in June, feeling good about my interactions with a lot of

staff people there, and impressed that they'd put up with me for almost three whole months.

I was shipped to Alderson, West Virginia. At a new place, you always have to start all over again, reconnecting (hopefully) with your personal property, making friends, developing your relationship with the institution. Alderson seemed initially to be more laid back than Fort Worth. I wasn't challenged on anything until the fifth day, when I was locked down for refusing to work. After two go-'rounds on that, I was left alone for nine whole days, my longest stretch in the general population at any federal prison.

But Alderson is a higher security prison than Fort Worth, and I had to respond to new restrictions there. The hardest one was that outgoing mail, which is all read, would not be sent out without an inmate registration number (assigned to you by the Bureau of Prisons at the time of your sentencing) in the return address; and I decided that I was unable to continue voluntarily providing that number. (A human being is not a number.) So I couldn't send out any mail for more than five months.

The other major restriction for me was that, though you could move freely around the grounds at many times and under many circumstances, you were required to sign out every time you left your 'cottage'. I was unwilling to do that routinely (though willing when it seemed to serve some purpose), and that became the primary issue on which the prison confronted me. Once I had been punished a time or two for refusing, the lieutenants began to track me. If they saw me in the dining hall or in the grounds, they would call my cottage to ask if I were signed out (thus demonstrating, to my mind, how unnecessary signing out was, since my whereabouts were already known). The officer on duty would then challenge me when I returned, and write me up for refusing an order to sign out. I would be locked up, sentenced to punishment status for as many as 21 days at a time (it could, legally, have been as many as 30), and lose some more 'good' days. It was soon unusual for me to stay in the general population for more than a day or two at a time.

I also continued to get locked up occasionally for refusing to work (if I were on the compound long enough to be given an assignment) and once for simply declining the physical exam. But I wasn't transferred, for which I'm thankful. I spent six months at Alderson, in and out of detention (mostly in), losing all but the last three weeks of my 'good' time, and growing in relationships with a lot of staff people, as well as inmates. You become well-known when you decline to co-operate and refuse to change. All sorts of people try to talk you out of your position, which leads to many opportunities for dialogue. You discover that there are people who care, even though their jobs don't give them many ways to express it. And you bear the pain of being punished by people who you know care, and of being punished for trying to do what's right in the midst of much that's wrong and that's careless.

The lieutenant motioned me over as I passed near him with my tray in the dining hall.

'Miss Haines, if you have time this afternoon, could you come by and see me in my office?'

I was charmed. I had always liked that particular lieutenant, from whom I felt some personal concern, and there was something chivalrous about the way he'd turned a command into an invitation. I was obviously in trouble. It could be because I wasn't signed out. But probably he had an incident report to issue me, which I knew had been written the night before when I'd refused to do a work assignment. This was the first time at Alderson that I hadn't been locked up on the spot, probably only because Davis Hall was over-crowded. His invitation was so unorthodox, though, that I had to make sure he meant it.

'Any time at all? You don't care?'

'No.'

'Okay, I'll be there.'

My friends all urged me to take a long walk. It was a glorious afternoon, and probably the last one for quite a while that I'd have the freedom to wander around in. But it *is* possible to receive an incident report without getting locked up until later on in the 'disciplinary' process. I wanted to find out what the lieutenant had in mind, and decided simply to ask him, trusting his already demonstrated willingness to respond to me humanly. He was no longer in the dining hall, so I'd visit him promptly and suggest that, if he intended to send me to Davis Hall, I'd rather come back later. At the very least, I was sure he'd let me go back to the cottage for my essential property. The risk of not bringing it with me was the concrete expression of my trust.

But the lieutenant wasn't in. I was told he'd just stepped out for a minute, so I decided to wait for a while, basking in the warm sun on a bench in front of the administration building.

A prison van drew up beside me, and an officer I didn't know jumped out.

'Are you Jennifer Haines?'

'Yes, I am.'

'Climb in. You're going to Davis Hall.'

I was neither particularly surprised nor upset, but I didn't move. I'd been trusting the lieutenant that I could take my property with me, which would greatly simplify subsequent interactions with my unit staff.

'May I pick up my property first?'

'No.'

'It's just around the corner, in cottage 12.'

'That's your counselor's responsibility.'

'My counselor never gets around to doing it.'

'I don't have time.'

'It's all packed.'

'All right. We'll swing around and pick it up.'

'I could walk over to get it and meet you there.'

The road was one-way, so I could probably reach the cottage as quickly on foot as the officer could by driving around three sides of a square, and I was eager for every last minute of sunshine.

But the officer was becoming impatient. 'Come along!' he ordered. So I climbed in. We drove around the first two sides of the square – and kept on going, up the hill toward Davis Hall.

I was incredulous. Even having seen officers manipulate inmates with blatant lies like that before, it had somehow never occurred to me that it could happen to me. I'm so scrupulously honest with *them*.

'You *lied* to me!' It was an indignant accusation. My property was no issue at all compared to the one of integrity.

'I needed to get you into the van. I figured you were sitting there in order to make a scene.'

I explained why I'd been sitting there. 'You said we'd pick up my property on the way, and we didn't. I won't co-operate with a lie.'

'I'll go down and get your things after I drop you off.'

'And how am I supposed to trust you to do that after you just lied to me? I'm not going to Davis Hall with you.'

This must have sounded rather humorous to him, since we were at that moment pulling up in front of the barbed-wire-topped fence and heavy electronic gate. But I was quite serious. He had seen the end of my co-operation. He could call for help to drag me into the building, and he could leave my property in cottage 12, but he couldn't get *me* to do anything else at all.

He climbed out of the van and walked around to my door, I sat still.

'I'm not going.'

'If you won't do this the easy way, we can do it the hard way.' But it must have been obvious to him that I had become immobile. He walked back around to his side, climbed in, and restarted the engine.

'We'll go see the lieutenant.'

'Okay.' That was fine with me.

We drove down the hill, continuing to talk. By the time we had nearly completed the square that took us back to the administration building, we had communicated enough to understand each other a little better perhaps. He stopped the van in front of cottage 12.

'I'll go in and get your property if you'll stay right here in the van.' I promised I'd stay, recognising the risk he was taking in choosing to trust me now. I told him where my things were. He found them, brought them out, and put them in the seat behind me. I thanked him. He mentioned easy ways and hard ways again; I told him I was okay; and we drove on past the administration building and back up to Davis Hall. I remembered how he'd said he didn't have time to get my property.

I was willing to walk into the building this time, and discovered when I got there that that was where the lieutenant had been, with my incident report, the whole time. He and I had a long and rather difficult conversation.

'Your staff is less ethical than *I* am.' He didn't deny it. As soon as I'd said it, I wondered why I was surprised.

And, finally, I had to know whether the *lieutenant* had lied to me.

'I came to see you this afternoon, and you weren't there.'

'I know I wasn't.'

'Did you expect me to come?'

'Yes.'

'What happened?'

'I was unexpectedly called up here.'

'And...?'

'And I saw the Old Man, who said that, even though we don't have space, because of who it is, you had to be locked up. So I sent my grounds person to pick you up.'

All right. That sounded plausible. Perhaps I could still trust the lieutenant. I felt very tired. They put me in a cell, and I was glad to be quiet for a long while.

My spiritual journey, of course, continues in prison. Hard as it may be, I'm content if I can let God use it for my growth and keep me loving. Caring and bearing pain are, after all, most of what it means to be a monk.

'A monk? But you're a nuclear resister, a witness for peace, a non-co-operator in federal prison.'

A monk is a person of prayer. Fortunately, that's a vocation you can carry with you. I do my best, and God is patient, forgiving, and faithful.

CHAPTER TWELVE

Civil Disobedience as Prayer

JIM DOUGLASS

Jim Douglass is a Canadian from British Columbia who now lives with his wife Shelley and son Thomas at Silverdale, Washington, near to the Trident nuclear submarine base at Bangor. A former teacher at the University of Hawaii and Notre Dame University, Illinois, he is the author of three books: The Non-Violent Cross; Resistance and Contemplation; *and* Lightning East to West. *In March 1972 he was arrested for illegal entry into Pacific Air Force Headquarters, Hickam Air Base, Hawaii, where he damaged secret military documents concerning the war in Vietnam. At his subsequent trial, the sworn testimony of a former Air Force sergeant contained the allegation that while stationed at Hickam Air Base he had witnessed the deliberate targeting of a Laotian hospital for obliteration bombing, as well as the targeting of many civilian objectives.*

The Douglasses work at the Ground Zero Centre for Non-Violent Action, where they strive to awaken awareness among workers at the Trident base to the responsibility that each of us has for the continuation of the arms race.

One way of seeing jail today is to regard it as the new monastery. In a society preparing for nuclear war and ignoring its poor, jail is an appropriate setting in which to give one's life to prayer. In a nation which has legalised preparations for the destruction of all life on earth, going to jail for peace − through non-violent civil disobedience − can be seen as a prayer. In reflecting today on the Lord's Prayer, I think that going to jail as a way of saying 'Thy kingdom come, thy will be done' may be the most basic prayer we can offer in the nuclear security state. Because we have accepted the greatest evil conceivable as a substitute for divine security, we have become a nation of atheists and blasphemers. The nuclear security state, USA or USSR, is blasphemous by definition. As members of such a nation, we need to pray for the freedom to do God's will by non-co-operation with the ultimate evil it is preparing. Civil disobedience done in a loving spirit is itself that kind of prayer.

On the other hand, civil disobedience can be done in a way that while apparently non-co-operating with nuclear war, ends up co-operating with an illusion that underlies nuclear war. In any attitude of resistance to the state there is a kind of demonic underside, power turned upside down, which wishes to gain the upper hand. Civil disobedience which is not done as prayer is especially vulnerable to its underside.

A simple truth at the root of non-violence is that we can't change an evil or an injustice from the outside. Thomas Merton stated this truth at the conclusion of one of his greatest books, *Mystics and Zen Masters*, as a critique of 'non-violence' as it is understood by its proponents in the Western world. Merton questioned 'the Western acceptance of a "will to transform others" in terms of one's own prophetic insight accepted as a norm of pure justice'. He asked:

'Is there not an "optical illusion" in an eschatological spirit which, however much it may appeal to *agape*, seeks only to transform persons and social structures *from the outside*? Here we arrive at a basic principle, one might almost say an ontology of non-violence, which requires further investigation.'

Non-violent non-co-operation with the greatest evil in history is still, according to Merton's insight, a possible way into illusion, a more subtle form of the same illusion that we encounter behind the nuclear build-up. Even in non-violent resistance, unless we accept deeply the spirit of non-violence, we can end up waging our own form of war and contributing to the conclusion we seek to overcome. Because the evil we resist is so great, we are inclined to overlook an illusion inherent in our own position, the will to transform others from the outside.

If one understands civil disobedience as an assertion of individual conscience over the evil or injustice of the state, the temptation to seek an 'outside solution' is already present. Conscience against the state sounds like spiritually based or 'inside solution'. We are, after all, stating our willingness in conscience to go to jail at the hands of the state that threatens an unparalleled evil. But our conscience set off against the nuclear state takes an external view of people acting on behalf of that state. And ultimately such a view externalises our own conscience.

In the acts of civil disobedience that I have done, I have never met 'the state'. In terms of my own ambition, that has been disappointing. I have met only people, such as police, judges, and jail guards who co-operate (and sometimes do not co-operate) with the evil of nuclear war in complex and often puzzling ways. I have never met a person who embodies the state or nuclear war. In their nuances of character, police, judges, and guards come from the same stew of humanity as do people who practise civil disobedience.

A spiritually based non-violence, one that truly seeks change from within, has to engage deeply the spirits of both sides of a conflict. Civil disobedience as an act of conscience against the state tends to focus exclusively on our own conscience as a source of change. Yet in the act of civil disobedience we meet particular people like ourselves, not 'the state', and the most enduring thing we can achieve through such an act is, in the end, our relationship to the people we touch and who touch us. Our hope should not be for any strategic victories over such representatives of the state, but rather loving, non-violent relationships with them in the midst of our arrests, trials, and prison sentences. The danger of seeing civil disobedience as an assertion of conscience over against the evil of the state is that it may get confused into an assertion against these particular people, so that we may never really see our relationship to them as primary. Making friends with our opponents — in the police, in the Pentagon, or in the Soviet Union — is our greatest hope of overcoming nuclear war.

A more fundamental question suggested by Merton is: Who is this 'I', this self, that is acting from conscience in civil disobedience? If civil disobedience accentuates, or heightens, this sense of self — if it gives it a sense of power — is that necessarily a good thing? Civil disobedience is often referred to today as a way of empowering its participants. For socially powerless people, non-violent civil disobedience can be a profoundly liberating way out of bondage, as one part of a larger revolution. But empowerment can also cover a heightened sense of an individual self and that may be a step into further bondage.

We who see ourselves as peacemakers — and don't we all? — would be deeply shocked if we could see the extent to which we act personally for war, not only in our more obvious faults, but even in our very peacemaking. Our intentions and actions for peace lead to war if they are based on a false self and its illusions. If the purpose of civil disobedience is to 'empower' such a self, it is a personal act of war.

The nuclear arms race summarises the history of a false, violent self — of many such false selves magnified in national egos — in an inconceivable evil. What the nuclear crisis says to us, as nothing else in history could, is that the empowering of a false self creates a crisis which has no solution, only transformation. We *can't* solve an arms race based on enormous national illusions, illusions which both exploit and protect an emptiness at the centre of millions of lives. Those illusions can only be cracked open to the truth and fear and emptiness at the core of each national pride, then revealed as truly reconcilable with their apparent opposites in the consciousness of another people.

Civil disobedience for the sake of empowering a false self is like the warring nation state on a smaller scale. Civil disobedience as that kind of empowerment is an attempt to solve personal problems and frustrations by externalising them in a theatre in which innocence confronts the evil of the nuclear state. But we are not innocent.

The greatest treason, as T.S. Eliot points out in '*Murder in the Cathedral*', is to do the right deed for the wrong reason. Civil disobedience in response to the greatest evil in history, done to empower a self which can't face its own emptiness, is the right deed for the wrong reason. Because of its motivation, it may also twist itself into the wrong deed. An ego-empowering act of civil disobedience will in the end empower both the self and the nuclear state, which while tactically at odds are spiritually in agreement. Such resistance, like the state itself, asserts power in order to cover a void. Civil disobedience, like war, can be used to mask the emptiness of a false self.

Civil disobedience as prayer is not an assertion of individual conscience over against the evil of the state. Protesting against something for which we ourselves are profoundly responsible is a futile exercise in hypocrisy. The evil of nuclear war is not external to us, so that it can be isolated in the state or in the Nuclear Train loaded with hydrogen bombs. The nature of the evil lies in our co-operation with it. What Merton is suggesting is that as we cease co-operating in one way with that evil, our well-hidden tendency is to begin co-operating

114

with it more intensely and more blindly in another way, defining the evil in a way external to us which deepens and hardens its actual presence in ourselves.

The power of the evil of nuclear war is not more than the power of our co-operation with it. There is no evil exclusively out there. The evil is much more subtle than that. This is why it continues to exist. When we accept responsibility for nuclear war in the hidden dimensions of our own complicity, we will experience the miracle of seeing the Nuclear Train stop and the arms race end. To paraphrase Harry Truman, the Bomb stops here.

Civil disobedience as prayer is not an assertion of self over against an illusion, but an acceptance of God's loving will because of our responsibility for evil: Not my will, but thine be done. The prayer of the Gospels, like the prayer of Gandhi, is at its heart an acceptance of what we don't want: the acceptance of our suffering out of love. Jesus and Gandhi are precise about what is meant by God's will in a world of suffering. Gandhi in summing up Jesus's life said: 'Living Christ is a living cross; without it life is a living death'.

To be non-violent means to accept our suffering out of love. The evil which causes suffering is an evil whose source is more deeply interior to ourselves than we have begun to understand. The prayer of civil disobedience which says, 'Not my will but thine be done' — by sending us to death or to that sign of death which is jail — is a recognition that in truth we belong there, and that we will in any event ultimately find ourselves there.

Civil disobedience as prayer is not an act of defiance, but an act of obedience to a deeper, interior will within us and within the world which is capable of transforming the world. 'Thy kingdom come, thy will be done.' To live out the kingdom of God through such an action is to live in a loving relationship to our brothers and sisters in the police, in courts, and in jails, recognising God's presence in each of us. It is also to accept responsibility for an evil which is ours: as we are, so is the nuclear state.

The two most violent places I've ever been in my life have been the Strategic Weapons Facility Pacific (SWFPAC), where nuclear weapons are stored at the heart of the Trident base, and the Los Angeles County Jail, where people are stored. I went to SWFPAC in order to pray for peace and forgiveness, standing in front of enormous concrete bunkers, the tombs of humankind — a prayer which took me in turn to the

L.A. County Jail (on the way to a more permanent prison), where ten thousand people are kept in tombs. The deepest experiences of peace that I have had have been in these same terrible places.

I believe that a suffering God continually calls us to be in such places for the sake of peace and justice. I believe that the kingdom of God is realised there. Civil disobedience as prayer is a way into that kingdom.

Epilogue

DONALD SOPER

The Revd. Dr Donald Soper (Lord Soper of Kingsway) has preached and worked for peace for sixty years. Although he is now 84 years old, and leads a busy life as a Methodist minister and a writer and broadcaster, he still preaches the Christian message in the open air every Wednesday on Tower Hill, in London, and every Sunday afternoon in Hyde Park. In his sermons as well as in his books (which include Will Christianity Work?, *Christian Politics, Calling for Action, and* Tower Hill 12.30*), Donald Soper returns many times to the theme of peacemaking, and the duty of Christians to work for justice and peace.*

During a conversation with Donald Soper that took place in July 1986, the Editors of this book asked him for his views on civil disobedience: can it be right for Christian peacemakers to break the law in their efforts to bring about disarmament? There follow extracts from the conversation.

Don Mason: The men and women who have contributed to this book have been imprisoned and treated as criminals (and so have we ourselves). Like our contributors, we would maintain that, where man's law and God's law are in conflict, we must obey God's law. What is your feeling on this point?

Donald Soper: If we can be sure of what is God's will in a particular situation (and discerning the will of God requires intelligence as well as fervour), then we really have no choice. If obedience to the will of God conflicts with the law of the land, then the law of the land cannot take precedence. There is an element of lawlessness in the

Christian life, because much of the law of the land falls short of Christian standards.

Don Mason: Mahatma Gandhi maintained that blind obedience to the law could be dangerous for democracy. The rise of Marxism in pre-war Germany bears this out: the holocaust could not have happened if the German people had been prepared to follow God's laws instead of Hitler's. Do you think that as society evolves, our ideas of what is acceptable will change?

Donald Soper: To talk of the law of God is to talk of something that is impervious to time, whereas the law of the land is constantly in a state of flux.

Catherine Robinson: Some peace activists, particularly in the USA, have intentionally damaged nuclear missile installations. To their critics, these protests are acts of violence; to the peace activists they are acts of symbolic disarming - of beating swords into ploughshares. Do you feel that the disarming of a nuclear missile can be regarded as an act of violence?

Donald Soper: I would draw a sharp distinction between violence applied to people, and violence applied to physical matter. I am prepared to be quite violent with a window that won't open! I see no ethical objection to the destruction of physical objects *per se*. But violence to people must be avoided at all costs.

Don Mason: In this book, Molly Rush says, 'The nuclear arms race is centrally a question of faith. It's a question of where one's trust goes: is it in this nation-state, with nuclear weapons, or is it in the God of power and might, the Creator, the one in whom we are to place our trust?' We feel that many Christians avoid asking themselves this question. But do you agree that it is an essential one for anyone professing Christianity to ask?

Donald Soper: Yes, without a doubt.

Catherine Robinson: Do you think that the Church is giving a sufficiently clear lead in these matters?

Donald Soper: No, I do not. But where Christians *are* active in opposing the growth of militarism in our society, their faith and love can act as the leaven in the lump of the world.

Don Mason: In a way, it could be said that the arms race and the Cold War have acted as a great catalyst for change, bringing together countless numbers of ordinary people to work for peace.

Donald Soper: God is not frustrated by evil! He can utilise it in ways that we cannot. 'The wrath of men can praise God.' I think that's in Psalm 76.

Catherine Robinson: But the sentences imposed by the courts on peace activists are often severe - as much as eighteen years in prison, in one instance in the USA. It is tempting to ask whether their actions are worthwhile. Father Paul Kabat, a contributor to this book, writing from prison in Minnesota, asks himself the question, 'What did you achieve?' Do you think that such actions achieve anything worthwhile?

Donald Soper: During sixty years of opposition to war, I have learned to be more concerned with obedience to what I see to be the truth than with calculating the results that might ensue from my actions. To be obedient to God is to release into his world agencies and powers for good that would otherwise have no access to the world. The consequences are not for me to predict. But in any case, if I believe that something is right, the question of whether I think it is likely to be successful is irrelevant...

THE EDITORS

Catherine Robinson is a mother and a Quaker. She lives in Oxford and works for a Third World charity. She grows vegetables and likes jazz. In 1983 she was arrested for her part in a peaceful protest against the extension of the USAF nuclear bomber base at Upper Heyford in Oxfordshire. She chose to go to prison because she could not agree to be 'bound over to keep the peace' — a peace enforced by nuclear weapons.

Don Mason is a graduate of both London and Oxford Universities and he works for the Medical Research Council as an immunologist. He is married and has four children. He and his family live in Witney in Oxfordshire.

Like Catherine Robinson he was arrested in 1983 at a non-violent protest at USAF Upper Heyford and he elected to go to prison rather than pay the fine imposed by the court because he did not accept the court's verdict that his own action was unlawful.

He is a member of the Medical Campaign Against Nuclear Weapons and was one-time chairperson of his local peace group. He and his wife have been Quakers since 1984.